W9-BJO-919

GRADE ONE MATH

Practice for Grade One

Packed with Math activities!

TIME

MEASUREMENTS

TABLES

GAMES

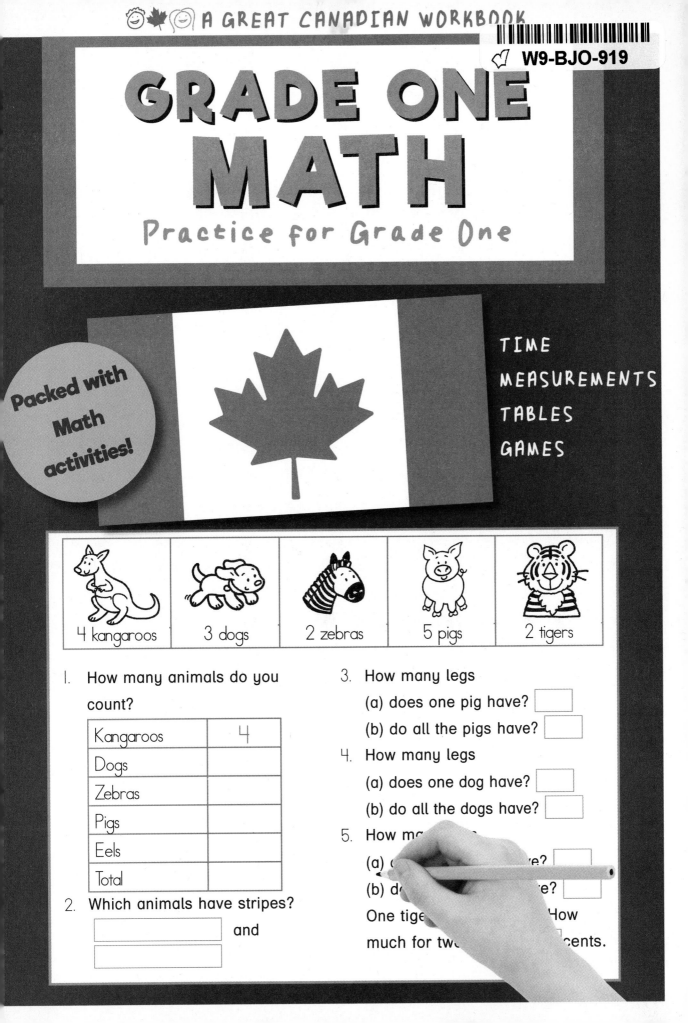

| 4 kangaroos | 3 dogs | 2 zebras | 5 pigs | 2 tigers |

1. How many animals do you count?

Kangaroos	4
Dogs	
Zebras	
Pigs	
Eels	
Total	

2. Which animals have stripes?

_____ and

_____

3. How many legs
   (a) does one pig have? ____
   (b) do all the pigs have? ____

4. How many legs
   (a) does one dog have? ____
   (b) do all the dogs have? ____

5. How m_____
   (a) _____ ?e? ____
   (b) d_____ ?e? ____

   One tige_____ How
   much for twe_____ cents.

Designed by Flowerpot Press
www.FlowerpotPress.com
PAB-0811-0168
ISBN: 978-1-4867-1479-7
Made in U.S.A/Fabriqué aux États-Unis

TABLE OF CONTENTS

The Great Canadian Workbook series from Flowerpot Press was developed with your child's success and enjoyment in mind. The activities are carefully organized to progress in a logical manner, but also varied to keep children motivated and entertained. The series is sure to appeal to the needs of all children, whether they need some extra practice or want a chance to work ahead. The journey through an individual workbook is easy to follow, and the content and complexity of each level builds on the previous workbook and flows naturally into the next.

Grade One Math is the fourth mathematics workbook in the series. It is ideal for children who have a basic understanding of math concepts like ordinal and cardinal numbers and addition and subtraction. Your child will begin by learning how to count up to 100, and by the end of the workbook they will be able to tell time, measure length, work with fractions and currency, and recognize 3-D shapes.

The learning adventure doesn't end here. Continue to develop your child's skills and love of learning with the other workbooks in the Great Canadian Workbook series:

1 2 3 4 5 6 7 8 9 10

11 12 13 14 15 16 17 18 19 20

21 22 23 24 25 26 27 28 29 30

31 32 33 34 35 36 37 38 39 40

41 42 43 44 45 46 47 48 49 50

51 52 53 54 55 56 57 58 59 60

61 62 63 64 65 66 67 68 69 70

71 72 73 74 75 76 77 78 79 80

81 82 83 84 85 86 87 88 89 90

91 92 93 94 95 96 97 98 99 100

Learning Goal: Learn to count from zero to one hundred.

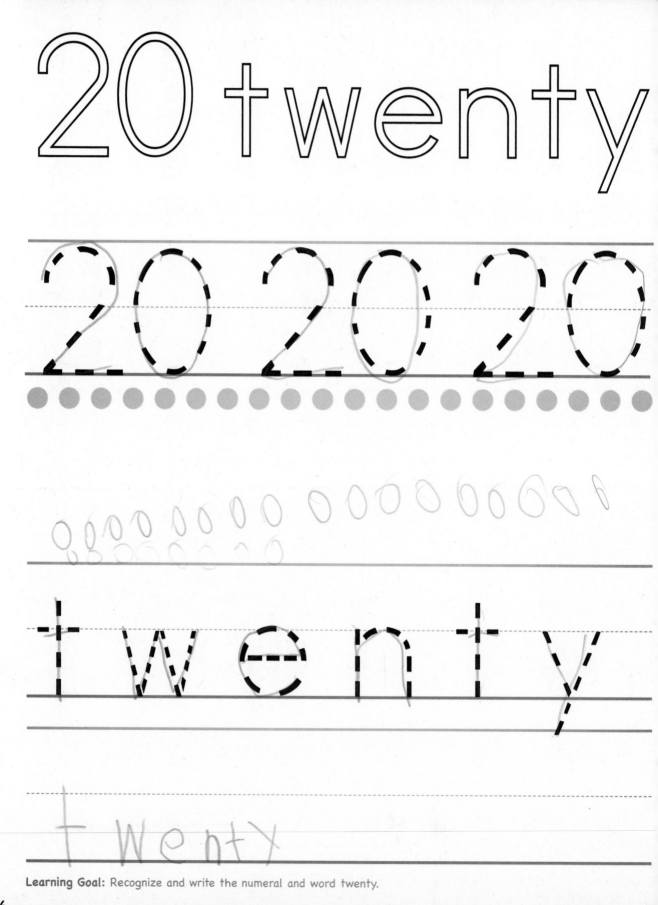

Learning Goal: Recognize and write the numeral and word twenty.

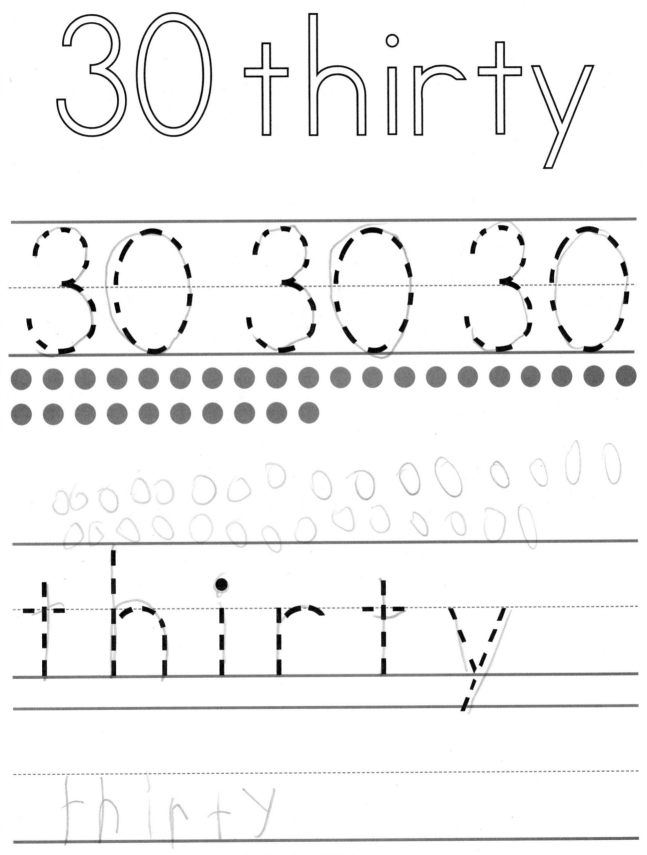

30 thirty

30 30 30

thirty

thirty

Learning Goal: Recognize trand write the numeral and word thirty.

40 forty

Learning Goal: Recognize tand write the numeral and word forty.

8

Use your finger to trace the numeral and word at the top of the page. Then practice writing the word on your own.

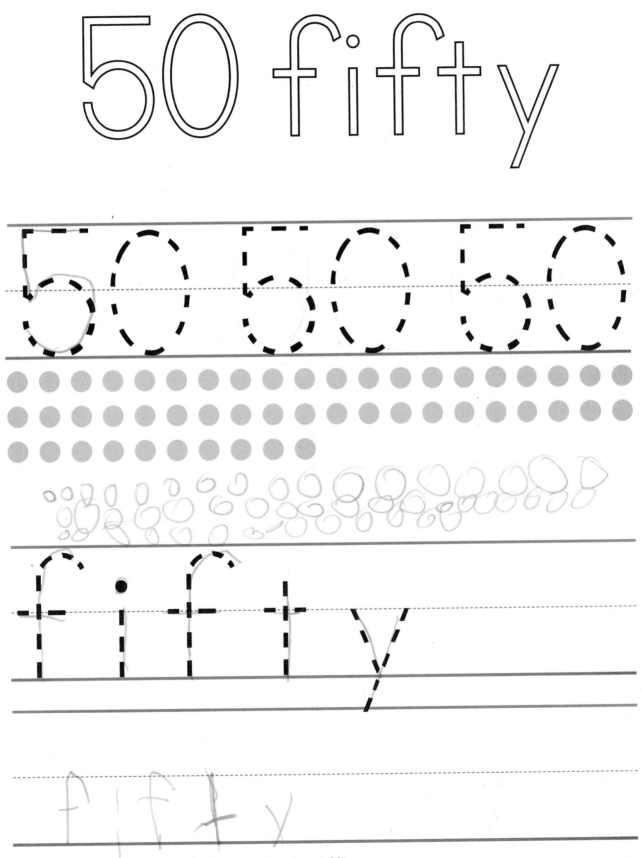

Learning Goal: Recognize and write the numeral and word fifty.

9

Use your finger to trace the numeral and word at the top of the page. Then practice writing the word on your own.

60 sixty

Learning Goal: Recognize and write the numeral and word sixty.

10

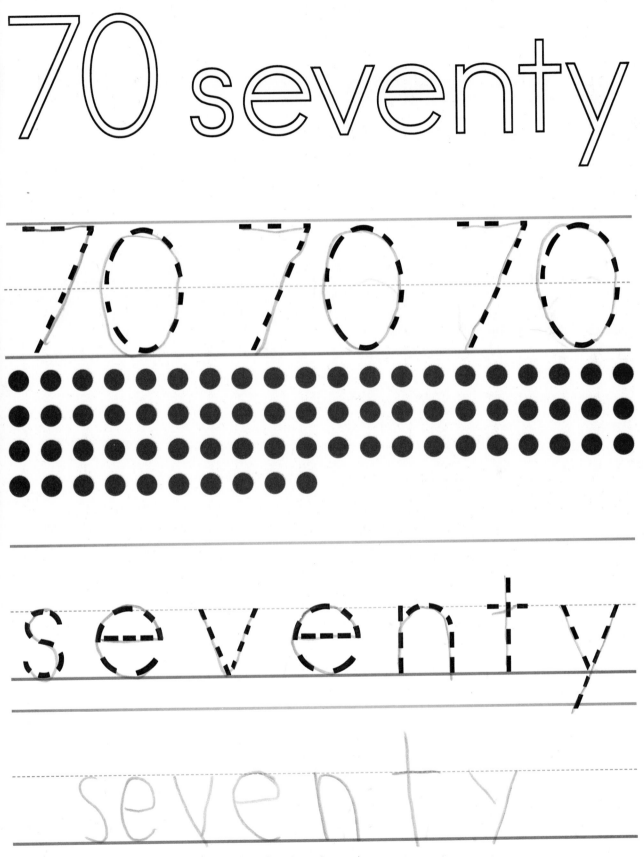

Learning Goal: Recognize and write the numeral and word seventy.

Use your finger to trace the numeral and word at the top of the page. Then practice writing the word on your own.

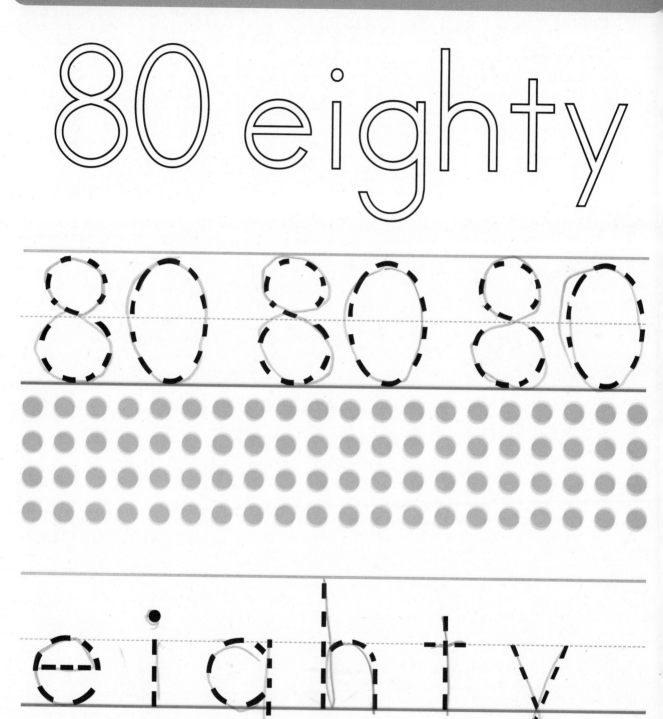

80 eighty

Learning Goal: Recognize and write the numeral and word eighty.

Use your finger to trace the numeral and word at the top of the page. Then practice writing the word on your own.

Learning Goal: Recognize and write the numeral and word ninety.

13

100   one hundred

Learning Goal: Recognize and write the numeral and word one hundred.

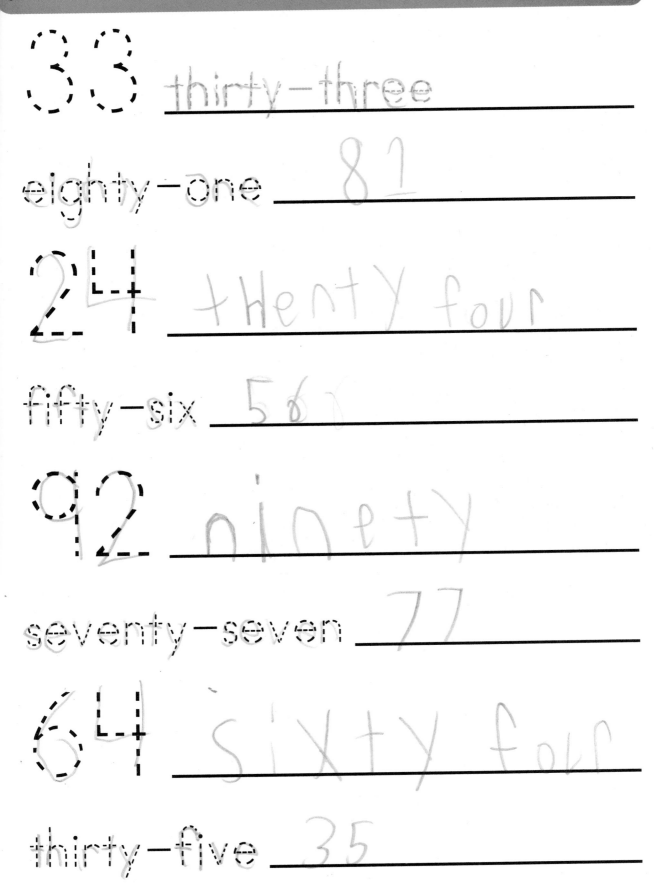

33 thirty-three

eighty-one 81

24 twenty four

fifty-six 56

92 ninety

seventy-seven 77

64 sixty four

thirty-five 35

Learning Goal: Practice writing numerals and words up to one hundred.

fifty-six

ninety-nine

sixty-one

seventy-nine

forty-two

eighty-four

twenty-three

thirty-nine

eighty

61

42

84

56

39

80

99

23

79

Learning Goal: Recognize numerals and words up to one hundred.

Draw a line to match the words to the correct numeral.

seventy-four

one hundred

sixty-five

thirty-three

fifty-one

eighty-eight

forty-eight

ninety-seven

twenty-nine

100

88

74

97

65

33

29

51

48

Learning Goal: Recognize numerals and words up to one hundred.

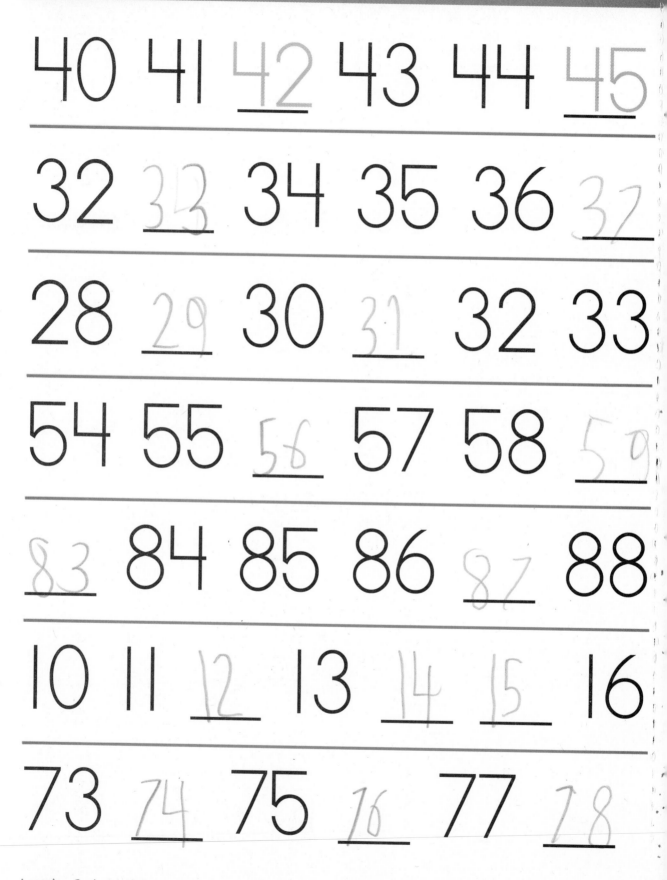

40 41 42 43 44 45

32 33 34 35 36 37

28 29 30 31 32 33

54 55 56 57 58 59

83 84 85 86 87 88

10 11 12 13 14 15 16

73 74 75 76 77 78

Learning Goal: Complete sequences with numbers up to one hundred.

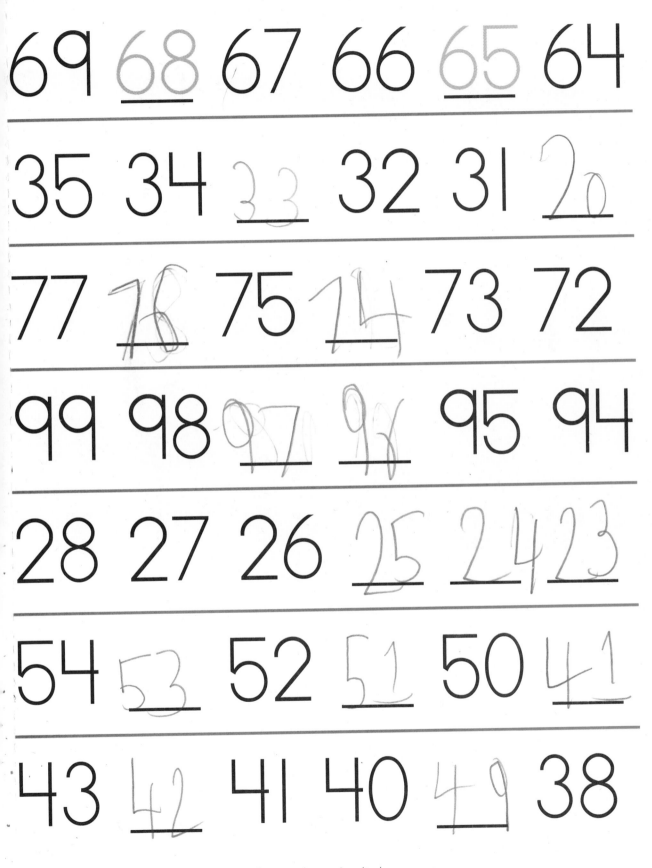

69 _68_ 67 66 _65_ 64

35 34 _33_ 32 31 _30_

77 _76_ 75 _74_ 73 72

99 98 _97_ _96_ 95 94

28 27 26 _25_ _24_ _23_

54 _53_ 52 _51_ 50 _49_

43 _42_ 41 40 _49_ 38

Learning Goal: Complete sequences with numbers up to one hundred.

Fill in the missing numbers on the snakes to complete the sequences.

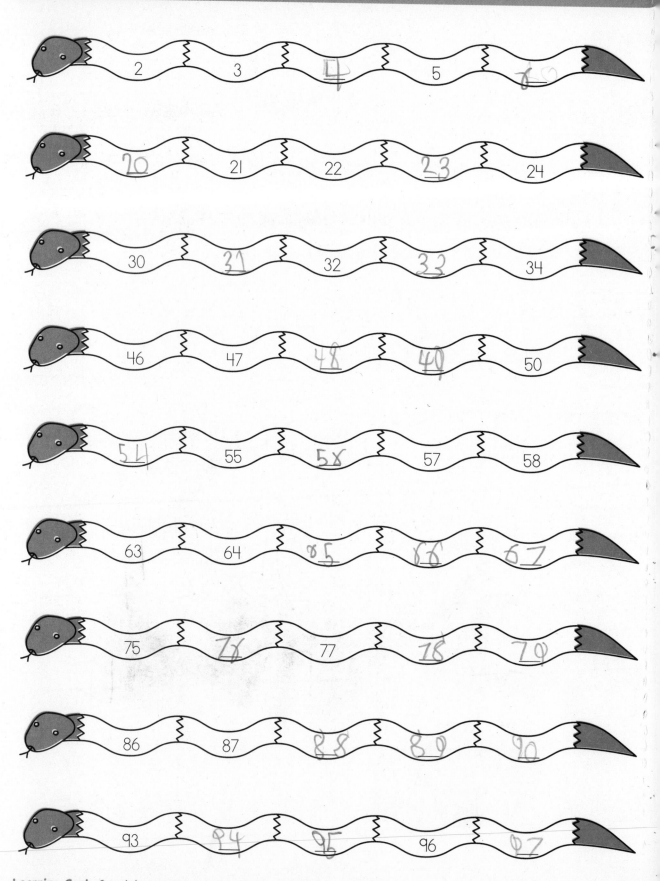

Snake 1: 2, 3, 4, 5, 6

Snake 2: 20, 21, 22, 23, 24

Snake 3: 30, 31, 32, 33, 34

Snake 4: 46, 47, 48, 49, 50

Snake 5: 54, 55, 56, 57, 58

Snake 6: 63, 64, 65, 66, 67

Snake 7: 75, 76, 77, 78, 79

Snake 8: 86, 87, 88, 89, 90

Snake 9: 93, 94, 95, 96, 97

Learning Goal: Complete sequences with numbers up to one hundred.

Circle all of the even numbers below.

Even numbers end in 0, 2, 4, 6, or 8.

12   13   14   15   16

22   23   24   25   26

30   31   32   33   34

41   42   43   44   45

52   53   54   55   56

Learning Goal: Recognize the difference between even and odd numbers. Correctly identify even numbers.

Circle all of the odd numbers below.

Odd numbers end in 1, 3, 5, 7, or 9.

1   2   3   4   5

19   20   21   22   23

93   94   95   96   97

82   83   84   85   86

67   68   69   70   71

Learning Goal: Recognize the difference between even and odd numbers. Correctly identify odd numbers.

Count the hockey pucks below. Then draw more pucks so there are 40 pucks total. How many pucks did you draw?

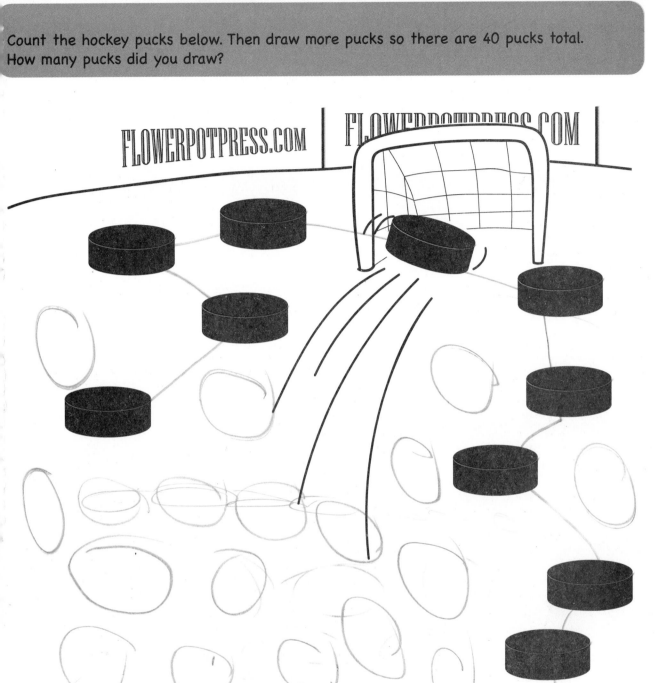

Learning Goal: Practice solving addition problems using only pictures.

Add the groups of pictures below. Write the number of items below each group to solve the problems. Then write the totals.

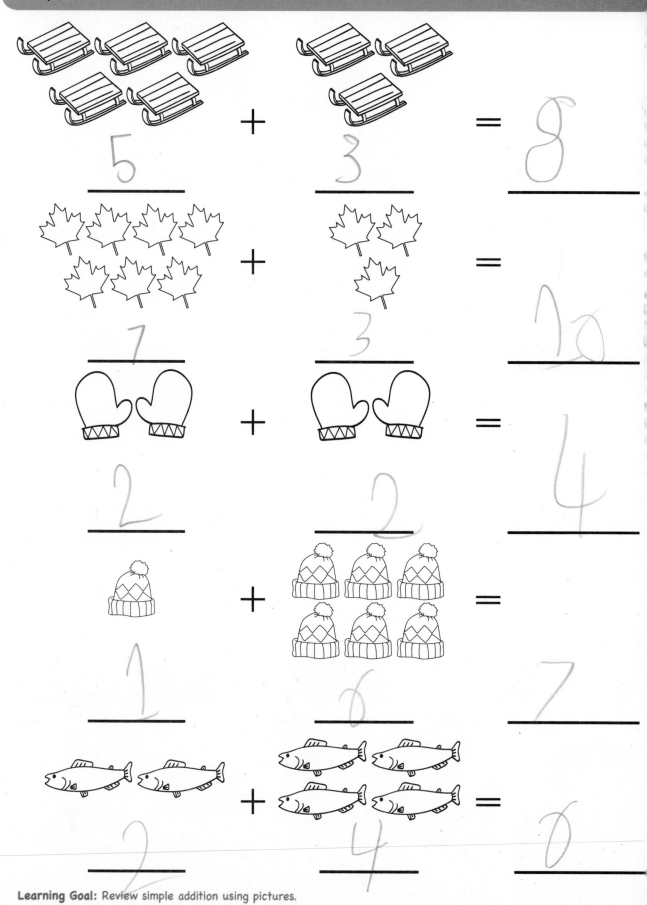

5 + 3 = 8

7 + 3 = 10

2 + 2 = 4

1 + 6 = 7

2 + 4 = 6

Learning Goal: Review simple addition using pictures.

Add the groups of pictures below. Write the number of items below each group to solve the problems. Then write the totals.

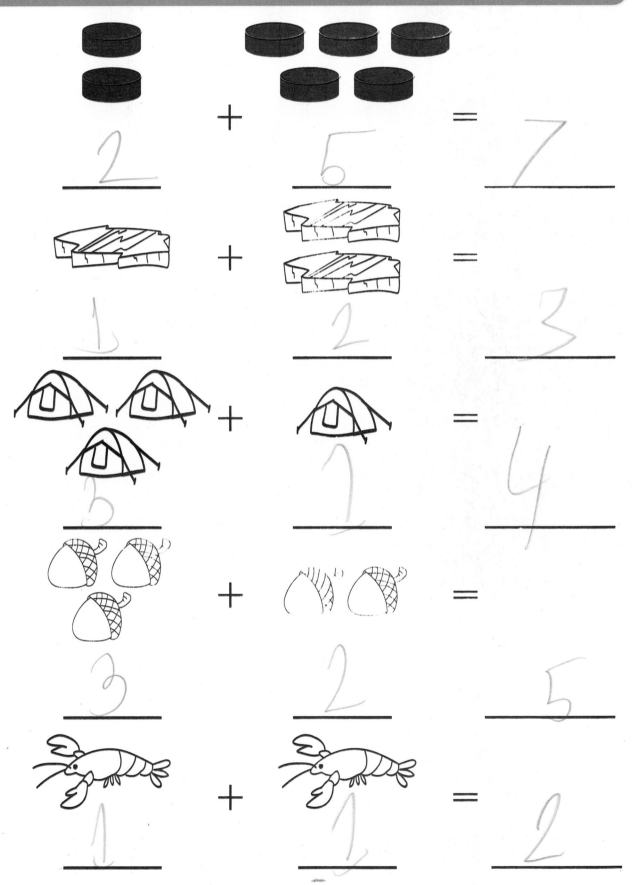

2 + 5 = 7

1 + 2 = 3

3 + 1 = 4

3 + 2 = 5

1 + 1 = 2

Learning Goal: Review simple addition using pictures.

$$\begin{array}{r} 7 \\ +\ 6 \\ \hline 15 \end{array} \qquad \begin{array}{r} 8 \\ +\ 3 \\ \hline 11 \end{array} \qquad \begin{array}{r} 6 \\ +\ 4 \\ \hline 10 \end{array} \qquad \begin{array}{r} 6 \\ +\ 5 \\ \hline 11 \end{array}$$

$$\begin{array}{r} 3 \\ +\ 4 \\ \hline 7 \end{array} \qquad \begin{array}{r} 2 \\ +\ 1 \\ \hline 3 \end{array} \qquad \begin{array}{r} 3 \\ +\ 2 \\ \hline 5 \end{array} \qquad \begin{array}{r} 2 \\ +\ 3 \\ \hline 5 \end{array}$$

$$\begin{array}{r} 4 \\ +\ 2 \\ \hline 6 \end{array} \qquad \begin{array}{r} 1 \\ +\ 6 \\ \hline 7 \end{array} \qquad \begin{array}{r} 3 \\ +\ 2 \\ \hline 5 \end{array} \qquad \begin{array}{r} 6 \\ +\ 0 \\ \hline 6 \end{array}$$

$$\begin{array}{r} 2 \\ +\ 2 \\ \hline 4 \end{array} \qquad \begin{array}{r} 6 \\ +\ 0 \\ \hline 6 \end{array} \qquad \begin{array}{r} 3 \\ +\ 4 \\ \hline 7 \end{array} \qquad \begin{array}{r} 1 \\ +\ 1 \\ \hline 2 \end{array}$$

Learning Goal: Practice solving addition problems.

28

$4 + 4 = \underline{8}$ $6 + 4 = \underline{10}$ $9 + 9 = \underline{10}$

$5 + 3 = \underline{8}$ $6 + 3 = \underline{9}$ $6 + 6 = \underline{12}$

$10 + 6 = \underline{10}$ $5 + 5 = \underline{10}$ $5 + 7 = \underline{12}$

$7 + 5 = \underline{12}$ $4 + 3 = \underline{7}$ $5 + 5 = \underline{10}$

$5 + 4 = \underline{9}$ $8 + 5 = \underline{13}$ $9 + 4 = \underline{13}$

$4 + 8 = \underline{12}$ $9 + 2 = \underline{11}$ $8 + 7 = \underline{15}$

$3 + 10 = \underline{13}$ $7 + 8 = \underline{15}$ $7 + 7 = \underline{8}$

$6 + 10 = \underline{16}$ $8 + 10 = \underline{18}$ $6 + 9 = \underline{15}$

Learning Goal: Practice solving addition problems.

Solve the math problems below. Then colour the picture using the key.

1 = ■ 2 = ■ 3 = ■ 4 = ■ 5 = ■ 6 = ■

$$1 + 0 = 1$$

$$3 + 2 = 5$$

$$1 + 1 = 2$$

$$3 + 1 = 4$$

$$4 + 2 = 6$$

$$1 + 2 = 3$$

Learning Goal: Practice solving addition problems.

Count the maple leaves. Add leaves to the tree so there are 35 total.
Then colour the picture. How many leaves did you add?

Learning Goal: Practice solving addition problems using only pictures.

Colour 13 hot-air balloons. How many hot-air balloons are left?

Learning Goal: Practice solving subtraction problems using only pictures.

Colour the lily pads to make a path for the frog so he can get to the marsh. How many lily pads did you colour? How many lily pads are left?

Learning Goal: Practice solving subtraction problems using only pictures.

Subtract the groups of pictures below. Write the number of items below each group to solve the problems. Then write the totals.

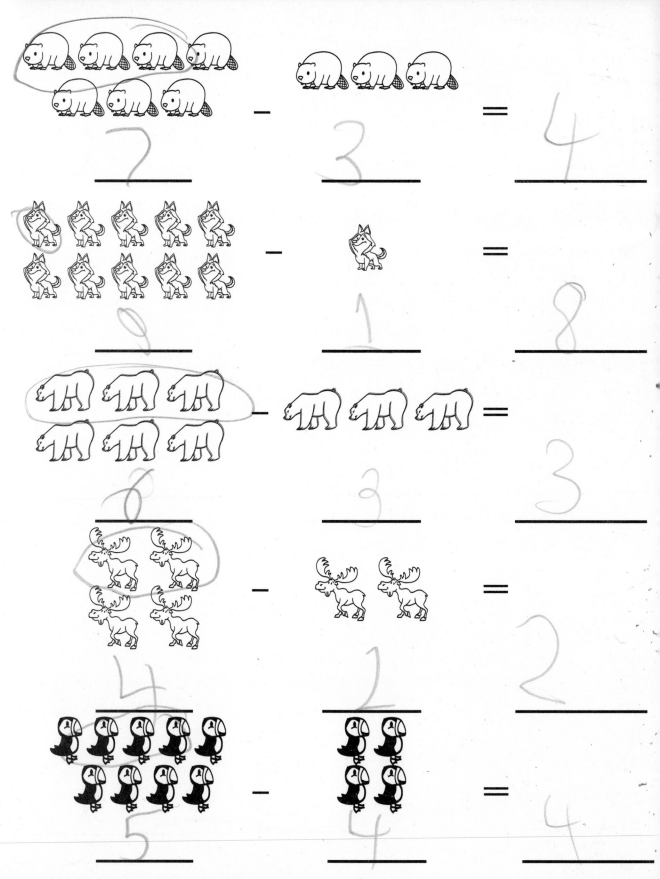

7
−
3
=
4

9
−
1
=
8

6
−
3
=
3

4
−
2
=
2

5
−
4
=
4

Subtract the groups of pictures below. Write the number of items below each group to solve the problems. Then write the totals.

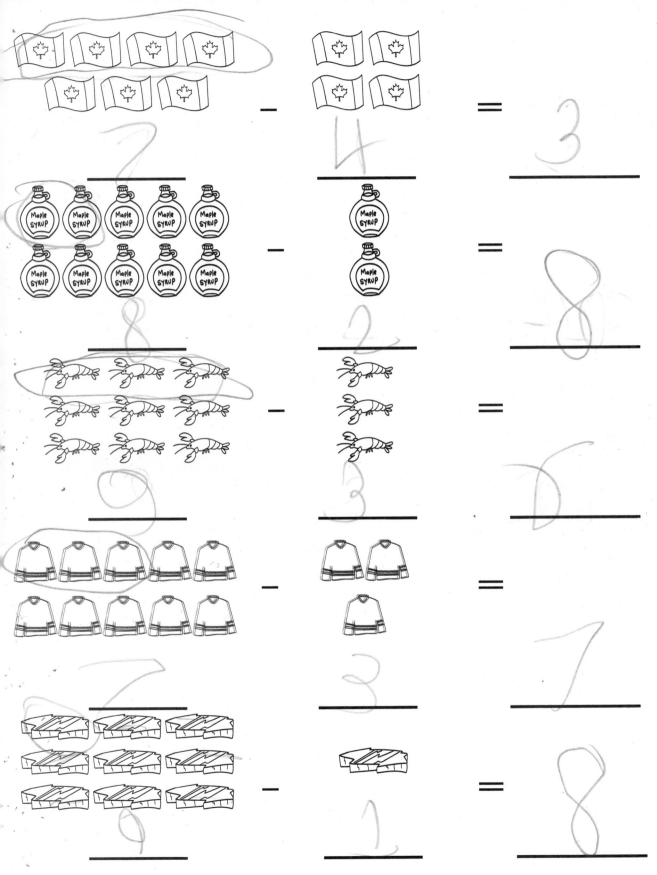

7   −   4   =   3

8   −   2   =   8

8   −   3   =   5

9   −   3   =   1

9   −   1   =   8

4	5	6	7
− 1	− 1	− 3	− 3
3	4	3	4

4	8	6	5
− 0	− 6	− 2	− 3
4	2	4	2

4	7	3	6
− 2	− 6	− 2	− 0
2	2	1	6

5	3	7	6
− 4	− 3	− 2	− 1
1	0	5	5

Learning Goal: Practice solving subtraction problems.

Solve the subtraction problems below. The first one is done for you.

$8 - 4 = \underline{4}$ $6 - 6 = \underline{0}$ $10 - 7 = \underline{3}$

$9 - 3 = \underline{2}$ $9 - 5 = \underline{4}$ $6 - 0 = \underline{2}$

$10 - 5 = \underline{5}$ $10 - 3 = \underline{7}$ $9 - 4 = \underline{5}$

$8 - 5 = \underline{3}$ $6 - 5 = \underline{1}$ $8 - 1 = \underline{7}$

$7 - 4 = \underline{11}$ $9 - 2 = \underline{7}$ $14 - 7 = \underline{7}$

$9 - 8 = \underline{5}$ $8 - 3 = \underline{5}$ $12 - 5 = \underline{17}$

$12 - 10 = \underline{2}$ $7 - 3 = \underline{4}$ $11 - 4 = \underline{2}$

$10 - 4 = \underline{2}$ $8 - 7 = \underline{15}$ $13 - 8 = \underline{15}$

Learning Goal: Practice solving subtraction problems.

Solve the addition and subtraction problems below.

$6 + 4 =$ __2__ $13 - 3 =$ __10__ $8 + 0 =$ __8__

$8 - 3 =$ __5__ $9 + 5 =$ __4__ $15 - 8 =$ __7__

$10 + 5 =$ __15__ $14 - 7 =$ __7__ $9 - 0 =$ __9__

$11 - 5 =$ __6__ $8 - 0 =$ __8__ $7 + 9 =$ __17__

$5 - 0 =$ __5__ $4 + 8 =$ __12__ $6 + 5 =$ __11__

$8 + 8 =$ __16__ $7 + 9 =$ __16__ $16 - 7 =$ __23__

$3 + 5 =$ __8__ $18 - 9 =$ __27__ $9 + 8 =$ __17__

$13 - 9 =$ __4__ $4 + 9 =$ __13__ $9 + 2 =$ __11__

$6 + 6 =$ __12__ $8 + 10 =$ __18__ $12 - 3 =$ __9__

$9 + 4 =$ __13__ $10 - 3 =$ __13__ $4 + 11 =$ __15__

Learning Goal: Practice solving addition and subtraction problems.

38

Solve the addition and subtraction problems below.

$4 + 5 = 9$ $12 - 4 = 8$ $9 + 1 = 10$

$13 - 8 = 5$ $8 + 9 = 17$ $12 - 8 = 4$

$5 + 5 = 10$ $15 - 6 = 9$ $13 - 7 = 8$

$12 - 0 = 12$ $8 - 1 = 7$ $8 + 3 = 11$

$15 - 7 = 8$ $0 + 9 = 9$ $4 + 7 = 11$

$9 + 9 = 18$ $8 + 5 = 13$ $16 - 4 = 12$

$8 + 6 = 14$ $17 - 9 = 8$ $4 + 12 = 16$

$14 - 6 = 20$ $6 + 9 = 15$ $8 + 0 = 8$

$4 + 9 = 13$ $8 + 13 = 21$ $15 - 4 = 11$

$5 + 9 = 14$ $13 - 4 = 9$ $9 + 10 = 19$

Learning Goal: Practice solving addition and subtraction problems.

Fill in the missing numbers to complete the addition problems below.

7 + 3   = 10   **10**

7 + 8 =   15
15 - 8 = 9

8 + 4 =   12

5 + 7   =   **12**

10 + 3   =   **13**

5 + 6 =   **11**

3 + 7   =   **10**

6 + 2 =   8

4 + 5   =   **9**

8 + 4   =   **12**

4 + 3   =   **7**

4 + 9 =   13

1 + 8   =   **9**

5 + 11   =   **18**

10 + 7   =   **17**

8 + 4 =   **12**

2 + 7   =   **9**

9 + 5 =   14

4 + 9   =   **13**

7 + 4   =   **11**

Learning Goal: Practice solving addition problems.

40

Fill in the missing numbers to complete the addition problems below.

$7 + 3 = 10$

$5 + 6 = 11$

$2 + 4 = 6$

$7 + 5 = 12$

$6 + 8 = 14$

$0 + 6 = 6$

$10 + 10 = 20$

$9 + 6 = 6$

$3 + 6 = 9$

$6 + 7 = 13$

$2 + 0 = 2$

$6 + 4 = 10$

$8 + 6 = 14$

$9 + 3 = 12$

$9 + 8 = 17$

$9 + 7 = 16$

$5 + 7 = 12$

$8 + 7 = 15$

$7 + 4 = 11$

$8 + 6 = 14$

Learning Goal: Practice solving addition problems.

41

6 dogs are pulling the dog sled. 6 more are added to make the sled go faster. How many dogs are pulling the sled total?

12

The hockey player skated around the rink 7 times. Then he decided to skate around 2 more times. How many times did he skate around the rink total?

9

3 friends were playing on the playground. 5 more friends joined. How many friends are on the playground now?

8

Aaron saw 3 snakes slithering in the grass. Then 2 more snakes slithered by. How many snakes did Aaron see?

5

There are 2 polar bear cubs playing on the ice. Then the mother polar bear joins them. How many polar bears are on the ice total? _____

Learning Goal: Practice solving addition word problems.

A mother goose was floating on Lake Ontario with her 6 goslings. How many geese are there total?

_____

There are 8 pine trees near the lake. My friends and I planted 7 new pine trees. How many pine trees are there near the lake total?

14
_____

There were 13 frogs jumping by the pond yesterday. Today another 4 frogs joined the fun. How many frogs are there total?

17
_____

$4 + 8 + 2 = 14$

Annie found 4 blue seashells, 8 yellow seashells, and 2 red seashells on the beach. How many seashells did Annie find?

14
_____

There are 16 strawberries and 2 bananas in the bowl. How many pieces of fruit are the in the bowl?

18
_____

Learning Goal: Practice solving addition word problems.

Al's dog Bo dug up nine bones and brought them inside. Later he found one shoe and five acorns and brought them inside. How many things did Bo bring inside?

14

The beaver found nine sticks for his dam. He then found four more sticks and three rocks. How many items does he have for his dam?

Amanda saw a lot of animals on her safari. She saw three monkeys, two lions, six giraffes, and four elephants. How many animals did Amanda see while on safari?

8

Nine kids got on the bus at 8:00 a.m. Four more kids got on the bus at 8:30 a.m. How many kids were on the bus at 8:30 a.m.?

$9 + 4 = 13$

12

Seven kids arrived for hockey practice at 5:30 p.m. Five more kids arrived at 6:00 p.m. How many kids were at practice at 6:00 p.m.?

$7 + 5$

Learning Goal: Practice solving addition word problems.

There are three deer in the forest with three points on each of their antlers (nine points total). Then a new deer with antlers with three points joins the other deer. How many points total do all the deer have?

15

The friends on the boat saw sixteen whales and seven sharks. A little while later they saw six dolphins. How many total animals did they see?

23

Five friends are going sledding. Ike brought three sleds to the hill. Eli brought one sled. Dana brought zero sleds. How many more sleds do they need so each person has a sled?

4

Kelly and her ten friends want to go ice-skating. How many helmets will they need?

11

There were sixteen moose in the forest. Later four more moose joined. How many moose are there now?

2

Learning Goal: Practice solving addition word problems.

Two hikers see 6 deer in the forest. Then 2 deer run away. How many deer are left?

_8_

Jessica bought 10 ice cream cones for her party. 4 ice cream cones melted. How many are left?

_14_

6 birds are in the tree. 2 birds fly away. How many birds are left?

_8_

There are 4 friends jumping rope in the park. 3 friends go home to do their homework. How many friends are left in the park?

_7_

There are 9 people rollerskating in the park. Then 2 people skate away. How many people are still skating in the park?

_11_

Learning Goal: Practice solving subtraction word problems.

T.J. and his friends ordered 8 pizzas. They ate 2 of them. How many pizzas are left?

____10

The hockey player had 17 pucks. He shot 6 pucks at the goal. How many pucks does he have left?

23

Andy could see 12 fish swimming in the lake. 4 fish swam away. How many fish are left?

16

Lucy bought 11 pieces of candy from the candy store. She ate 2 of them on the way home. How many pieces of candy does she have left?

13

The tree has 14 maple leaves on its branches. 2 leaves fall off. How many leaves are left?

____16

Learning Goal: Practice solving subtraction word problems.

Ten kids got on the bus after school. When Jenny gets off the bus there are only four kids left. How many kids had gotten off the bus before Jenny?

5

_____

Eight red cars drove by Kate's house. Then five green cars drove by. How many more red cars than green cars drove by?

13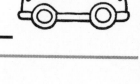

_____

There are four red fish, three green fish, and two blue fish in the sea. Two of the red fish swim away. How many fish are left?

7

_____

Six teammates go to the locker room to put on their jerseys. Everyone brought a jersey except one person. How many total jerseys are there?

0

_____

There are fourteen boats on the lake. Five boats go back to the dock. How many boats are still on the lake?

18

_____

Learning Goal: Practice solving subtraction word problems.

Solve the word problems below. Write your answers on the lines.

There are four polar bears next to the icy water. One polar bear dives in and one polar bear walks away. How many polar bears are left? _5_

Two friends each bring a dessert to the party. The first friend brings twenty cookies. The second friend brings four cakes. How many more cookies are there than cakes? 2+20+4=26 _28_

Twelve hockey players are playing. Each player has one stick. During the game two sticks break. How many sticks are left at the end of play? 12+2= _14_

We saw four bear cubs on our hike. One cub was sleeping and two of the cubs were playing. How many cubs were not sleeping or playing? _3_

Jo and her seven friends wanted to play in the snow. They each put on a pair of mittens, but one of them lost their pair. How many pairs of mittens do they have left? _8_

Learning Goal: Practice solving subtraction word problems.

Emma is throwing a party. She is inviting 12 people from her class, 5 people from her hockey team, and 8 people from her dance class. How many people will be at Emma's party including Emma?

$12 + 5 + 8 =$

20

Billy and his friends are going camping. They are bringing 1 tent, 7 snacks, 3 sleeping bags, 6 water bottles, and 3 jackets. How many items total are they bringing to the campsite?

25

$20 + 3 + 5 = 55$

Joshua loves pancakes. One morning, Joshua's dad made him 20 pancakes. He ate 3 chocolate chip pancakes, 5 pancakes with maple syrup, 4 blueberry pancakes, and 1 banana pancake. How many pancakes are left?

55

Anna ate 6 cookies after dinner. The cookie jar has 7 cookies left. How many cookies were in the jar before Anna ate her cookies?

13

Learning Goal: Practice solving both addition and subtraction word problems.

Sarah and her friends want to go ice-skating. Sarah has twelve friends and seven pairs of ice skates. How many more pairs of ice skates will she need?

_18_

Jack is going to the playground for forty minutes. He wants to spend ten minutes playing baseball, five minutes on the slide, and fifteen minutes on the monkey bars. How many minutes will he be playing baseball and be the slide?

_55_

There are fourteen geese floating on the lake. Six geese fly away, three geese dive under water and one goose comes back to float on the water. How many geese are floating on the lake?

_19_

Megan is picking grapes. She picked nineteen grapes and then ate four of them. She then picked three more. How many grapes does Megan have now?

_23_

Learning Goal: Practice solving both addition and subtraction word problems.

Count the objects below and determine if the group on the left is greater than, less than, or equal to the group on the right. Write the correct symbol in the circle.

Less than: <   Great than: >   Equal to: =

Learning Goal: Learn the differences and practice writing greater than, less than, and equal to symbols.

Count the objects below and determine if the group on the left is greater than, less than, or equal to the number on the right. Write the correct symbol in the circle.

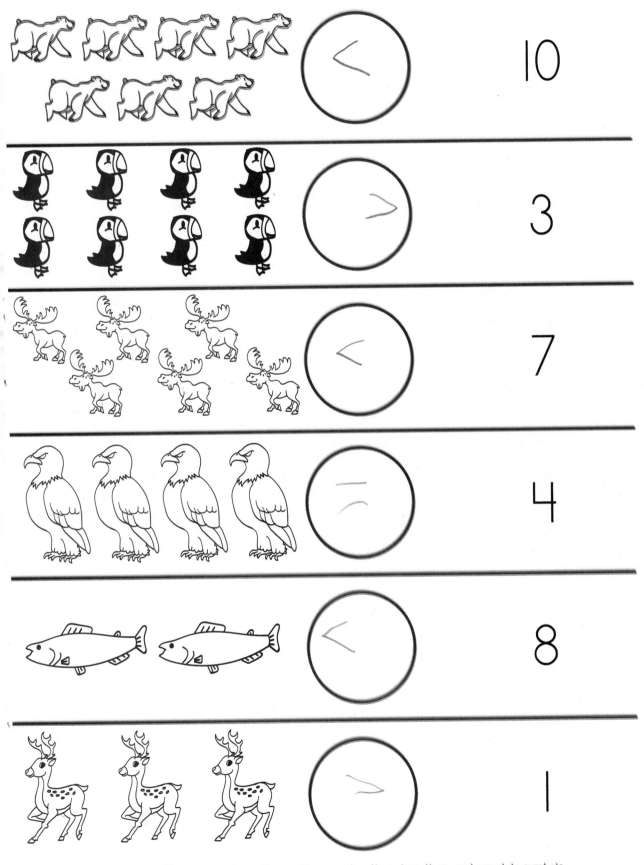

Learning Goal: Learn the differences and practice writing greater than, less than, and equal to symbols.

53

Use the key below to learn the different coin values. Then draw a line to match the coin to the correct name. The first one is done for you.

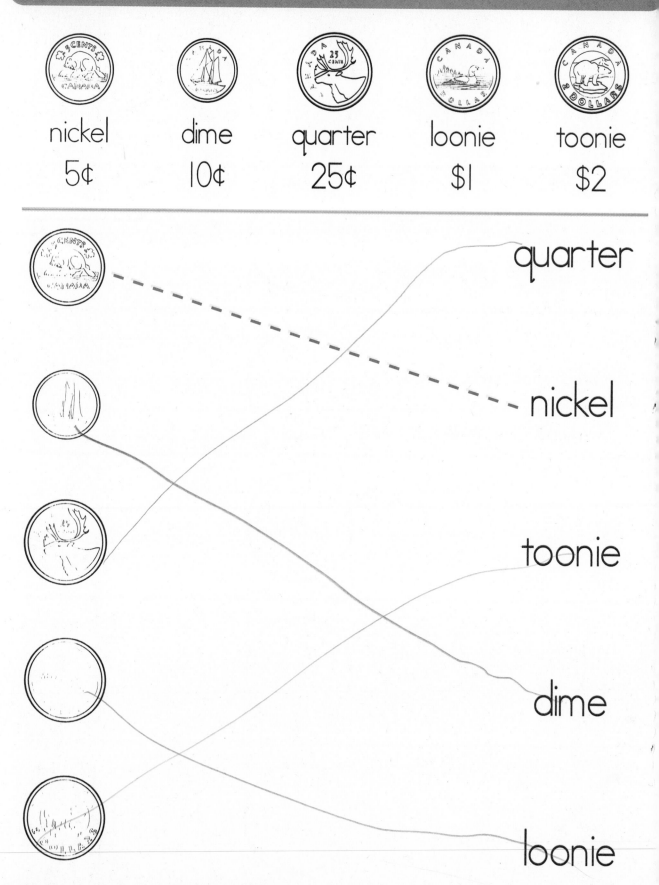

| nickel | dime | quarter | loonie | toonie |
| 5¢ | 10¢ | 25¢ | $1 | $2 |

quarter

nickel

toonie

dime

loonie

Add the coins below and write your answers on the lines. Include a $ symbol for values over 1 dollar and a ¢ symbol for values below 1 dollar. The first one is done for you.

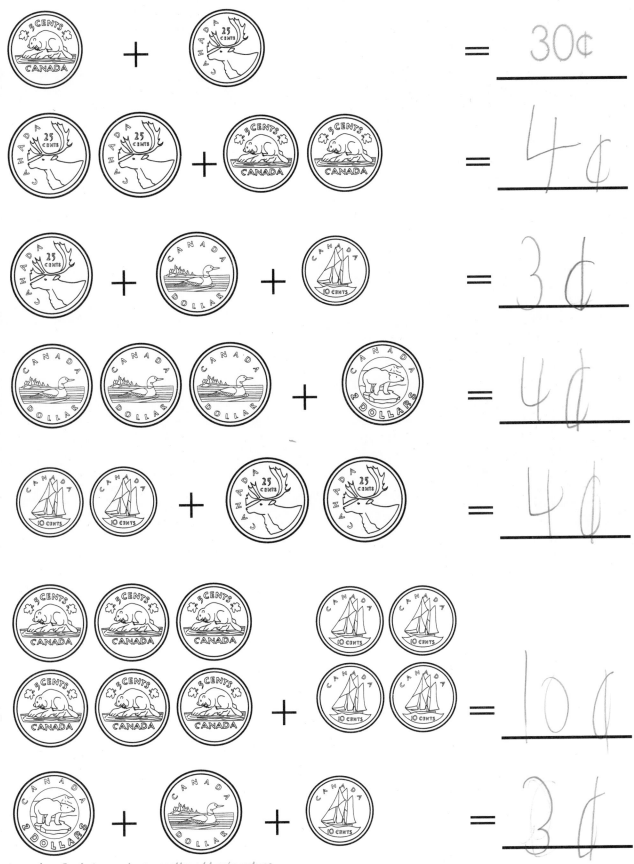

= 30¢

= 4¢

= 3¢

= 4¢

= 4¢

= 10¢

= 3¢

Learning Goal: Learn to correctly add coin values.

nickel   pime   quarter   bonle   tooni

Draw the coins you need to buy 3 ice cream cones.

ICE CREAM $1.50

Solve the word problem below.

Kelsey has 3 loonies, 4 quarters,
5 dimes, and 10 nickels. How many
ice cream cones can Kelsey buy
from the ice cream stand?

_____

Learning Goal: Practice solving word problems using coin values.

$2.50 $3.75 $4.50 $3.00

1. Susie wants to buy a train. How many quarters will she need? _____

2. Madison wants to buy a horse. How many dimes will she need? _____

3. Eliot and Kara have 3 loonies. Which item(s) can they buy? _____

4. Amy has 5 quarters, 5 dimes, and 15 nickels. Which item(s) can she buy? _____

5. Jennifer wants to buy the car. She has 4 quarters, 5 dimes, and 2 nickels. How much more money does she need? _____

6. Alex wants to buy the car and the train. How much money does he need? _____

7. How much money do you need to buy the doll, the horse, and the car? _____

Learning Goal: Learn to identify coin values and solve word problems.

Ben has 2 loonies, 6 quarters, 4 dimes, and 8 nickels. How much money does Ben have?

_____

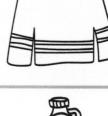

Sophia has 6 loonies and 4 toonies. How much money does Sophia have?

_____

Jacob has 15 dimes. He spent 9 of his dimes on candy. How many dimes does Jacob have left?

_____

Lily wants to buy a flower for her mom's birthday. Daisies cost $1.50. Lily has $9.00. How many daisies can she buy?

_____

Leah and Sofia want to each buy an ice cream cone. Ice cream cones cost $2.50 each. Leah has $2.00 and Sofia $1.00. Do they have enough money to buy two ice cream cones?

_____

Learning Goal: Practice solving word problems using coin values.

Owen and Adam have $11.00. They spent $4.00 on a chocolate cake and $2.00 on a vanilla cake. How much money do they have left?

_____

Ava wants to buy a teddy bear. The large teddy bear is $5.00. The medium teddy bear is $3.50. The small teddy bear is $1.50. Ava has $4.00. Which bear(s) can she buy?

_____

Mia wants to buy a toy train. Toy trains cost $5.00. Mia has 2 loonies and 3 toonies. How much money does she have? Does Mia have enough money?

_____

_____

Dan wants to buy a snack. He can buy apples for $4.00, chips for $3.00, or a sandwich for $5.00. Dan has 3 toonies, 6 quarters, and 5 dimes. How much money does Dan have? What can he buy?

_____

_____

Learning Goal: Practice solving word problems using coin values.

Use the clock to help you answer the questions below.

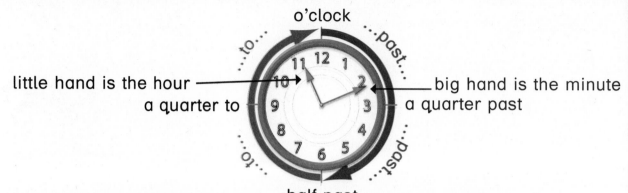

o'clock

little hand is the hour
a quarter to

big hand is the minute
a quarter past

half past

Match the times on the clocks to the letters. Write the correct letter on the lines below. The first one is done for you. (A) half past nine (B) five o'clock (C) half past four (D) half past eight (E) twelve o'clock (F) eleven o'clock (G) seven o'clock (H) two o'clock.

4:30 C

5:00

7:00

9:00

12:00

11:00

9:00

2:00

Draw the times on the clocks. The first one is done for you.

seven o'clock

one o'clock

half past ten

five o'clock

two o'clock

nine o'clock

half past six

half past four

half past eight

half past three

Learning Goal: Learn to tell time using analog clocks.

1:00   three o'clock

2:00   nine o'clock

10:00   twelve o'clock

9:00   one o'clock

12:00   five o'clock

5:00   two o'clock

3:00   seven o'clock

7:00   ten o'clock

Learning Goal: Recognize times when they are represented in digital form and when they are spelled out.

Draw a line to match the clock to the correct time. The first one is done for you.

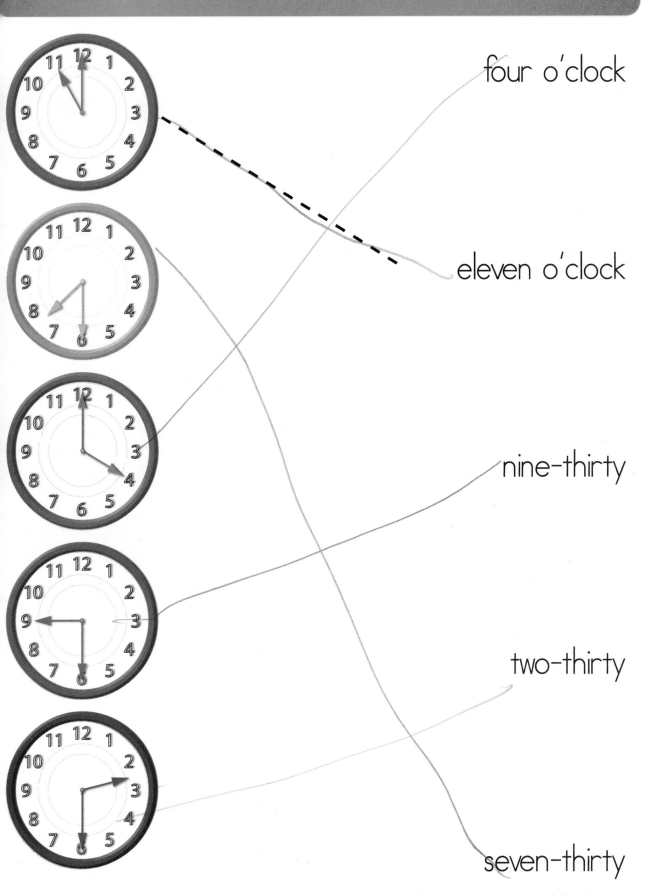

four o'clock

eleven o'clock

nine-thirty

two-thirty

seven-thirty

Learning Goal: Recognize times when they are represented on an analog clock and when they are spelled out.

eating breakfast

hockey practice

going to school

a.m.

AM

AM

going to bed

eating dinner

waking up

PM

PM

AM

Learning Goal: Learn the differences between a.m. and p.m.

Write the times in the box below in the correct category. The first one is done for you.

3:00 p.m.	10:00 p.m.	5:30 p.m.
9:00 a.m.	12:00 p.m.	10:00 a.m.
9:00 p.m.	1:30 p.m.	5:30 a.m.
1:30 a.m.	6:00 a.m.	8:00 p.m.

MORNING	AFTERNOON	NIGHT
5:30 a.m	10:00 PM	5:30 PM
9:00 AM	12:00 PM	1:00
9	1:30 00	8:00
1:30 AM	1:30 00	

Learning Goal: Recognize and properly categorize digital times.

Write numbers 1 through 8 in the boxes below. Write 1 for the shortest line and 8 for the longest line. The first one is done for you.

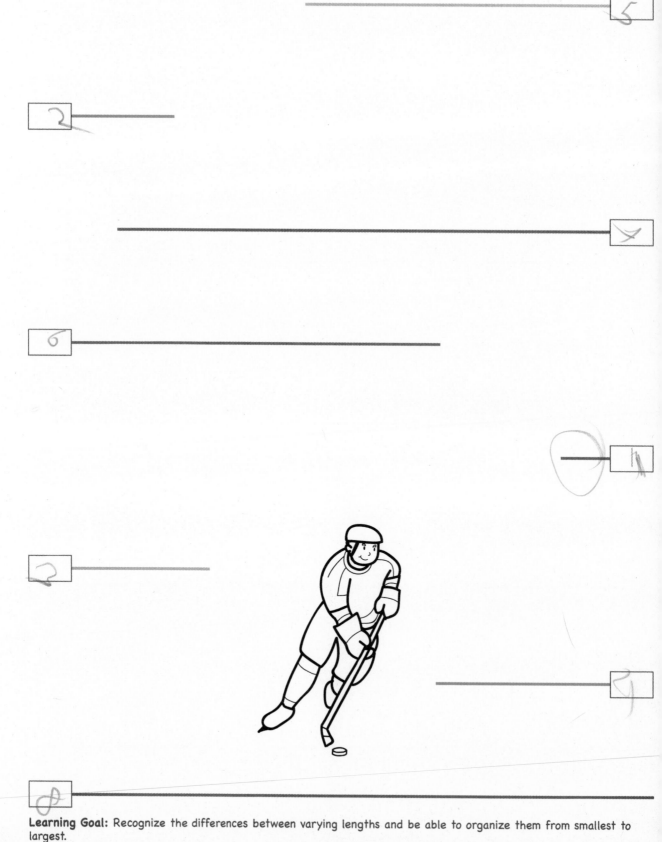

5

2

7

6

1

3

4

8

Learning Goal: Recognize the differences between varying lengths and be able to organize them from smallest to largest.

Write numbers 1 through 8 in the boxes below. Write 1 for the shortest line and 8 for the longest line. The first one is done for you.

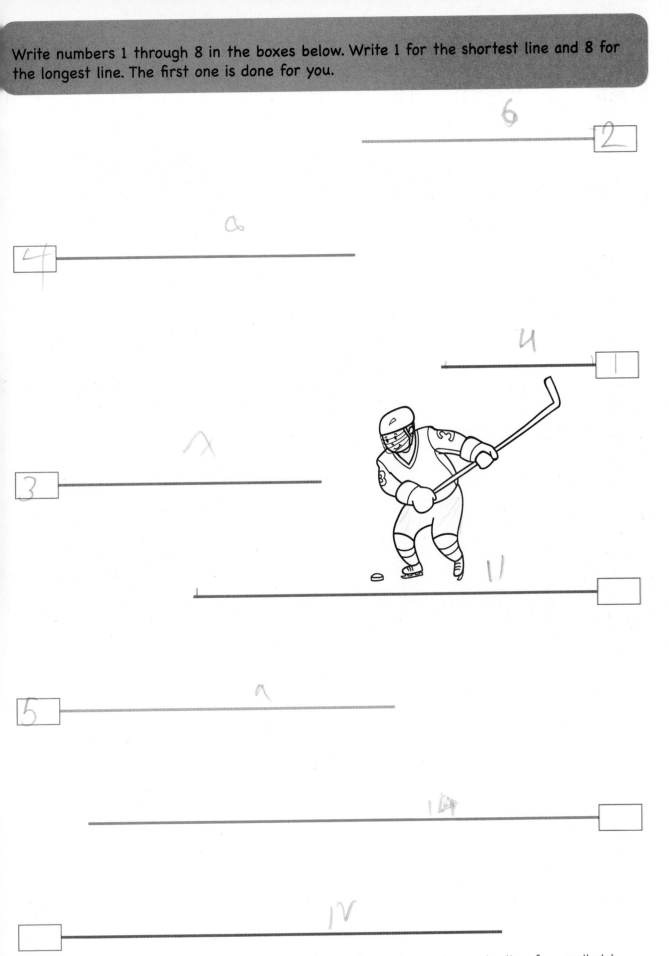

6

2

6

4

4

1

7

3

1

5

4

1

Learning Goal: Recognize the differences between varying lengths and be able to organize them from smallest to largest.

Use the ruler to help you measure the lines below. Write your answers in the boxes and use the number bank at the top of the page. The first one is done for you.

1	6	10	15
2	8	4	13

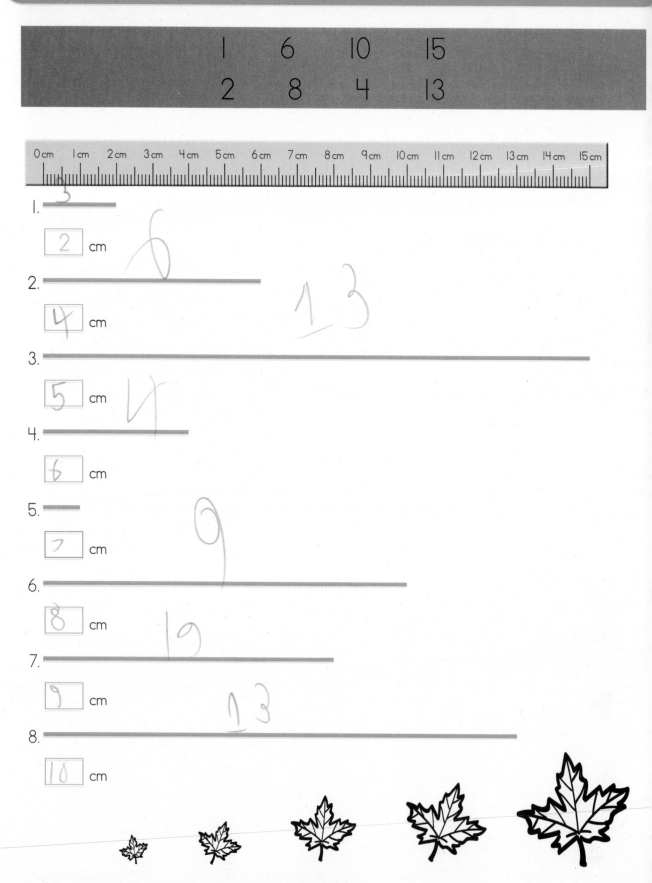

0 cm 1 cm 2 cm 3 cm 4 cm 5 cm 6 cm 7 cm 8 cm 9 cm 10 cm 11 cm 12 cm 13 cm 14 cm 15 cm

1.
[2] cm

2.
[4] cm

3.
[5] cm

4.
[6] cm

5.
[7] cm

6.
[8] cm

7.
[9] cm

8.
[10] cm

Learning Goal: Practice measuring varying lengths using a ruler.

Use the ruler to help you measure the lines below. Write your answers in the boxes and use the number bank at the top of the page. The first one is done for you.

7   12   5   9
14   11   8   3

0cm 1cm 2cm 3cm 4cm 5cm 6cm 7cm 8cm 9cm 10cm 11cm 12cm 13cm 14cm 15cm

1.
[7] cm

2.
[8] cm   130

3.
[9] cm   66

4.
[10] cm   130

5.
[11] cm   120

6.
[12] cm   120

7.
[13] cm   130

8.
[14] cm

Learning Goal: Practice measuring varying lengths using a ruler.

Use the ruler to help you measure the lines below. Write your answers in the boxes and use the number bank at the top of the page. The first one is done for you.

10　　5　　13　　15
1　　9　　8　　3

```
0cm  1cm  2cm  3cm  4cm  5cm  6cm  7cm  8cm  9cm  10cm  11cm  12cm  13cm  14cm  15cm
```

1. ▬

    | 1 | cm

2. ▬▬▬▬

    | 2 | cm

3. ▬▬▬▬▬▬▬▬▬▬▬▬

    | 3 | cm

4. ▬▬▬▬▬▬▬

    | 4 | cm

5. ▬▬▬▬▬▬▬▬

    | 5 | cm

6. ▬▬▬▬▬▬▬▬▬▬

    | 8 | cm

7. ▬▬▬

    | 7 | cm

8. ▬▬▬▬▬▬▬

    | 8 | cm

Learning Goal: Practice measuring varying lengths using a ruler.

70

Use a ruler to measure the length of each object. Write your answers on the lines below.

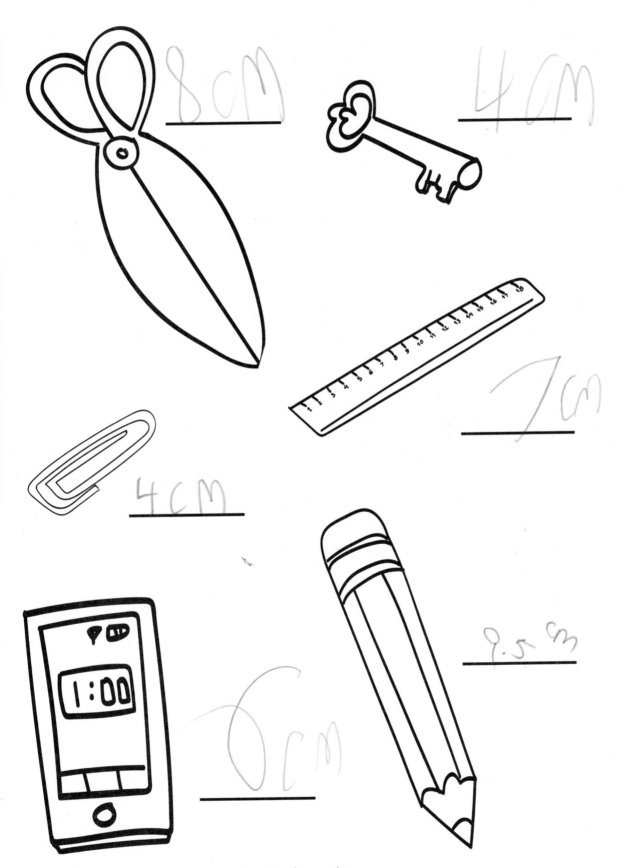

8 cm

4 cm

7 cm

4 cm

9.5 3

6 cm

Learning Goal: Practice measuring varying lengths using a ruler.

Draw a line to match the fractions to the correct shape representing that fraction. The first one is done for you.

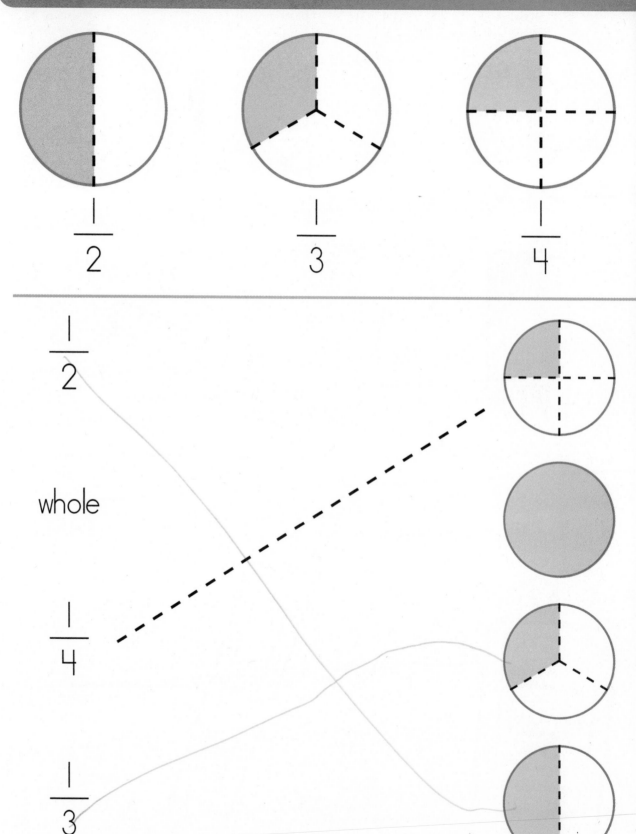

Learning Goal: Recognize fractions and be able to correctly match them to corresponding shapes.

72

Colour $\frac{1}{2}$ of each of the shapes below. The first one is done for you.

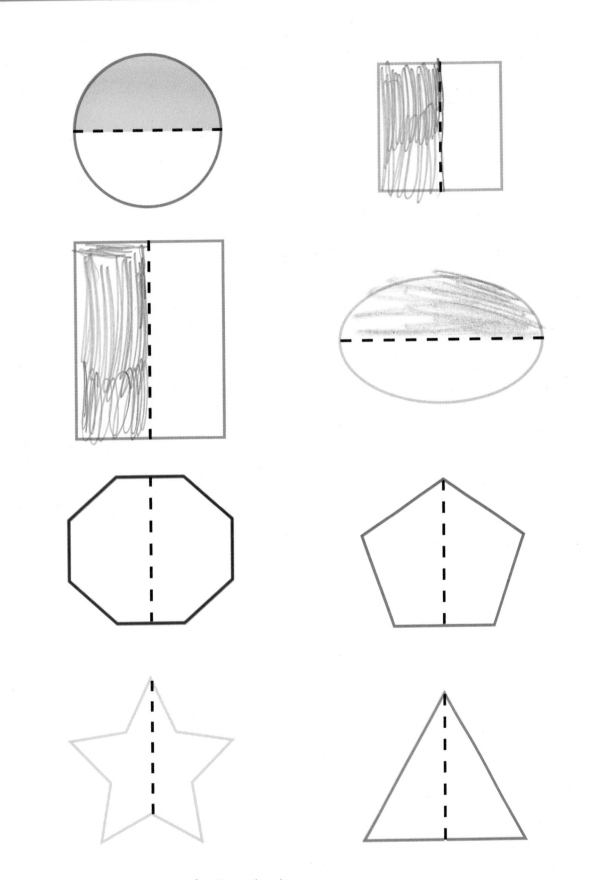

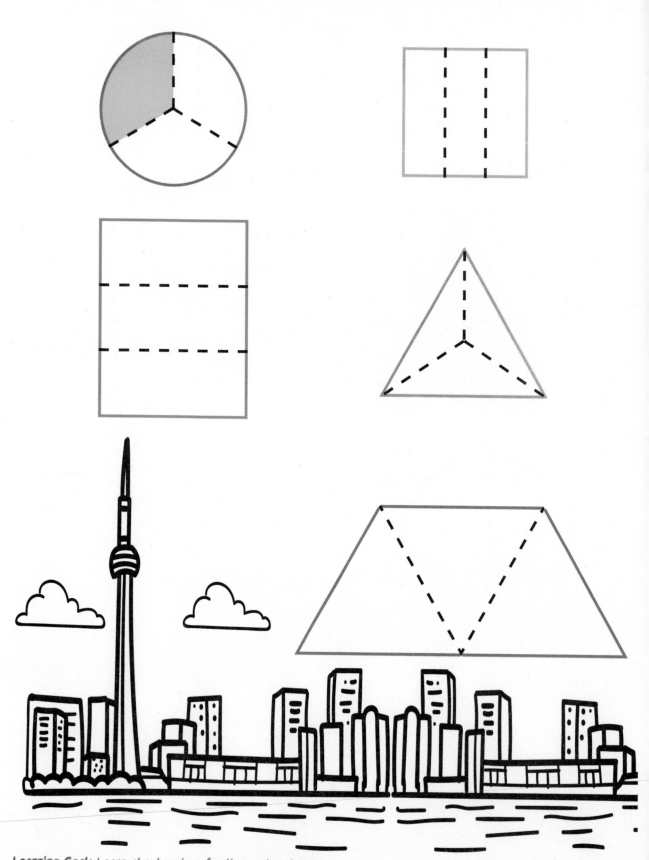

Learning Goal: Learn about various fractions using shapes.

Colour $\frac{1}{4}$ of each of the shapes below. The first one is done for you.

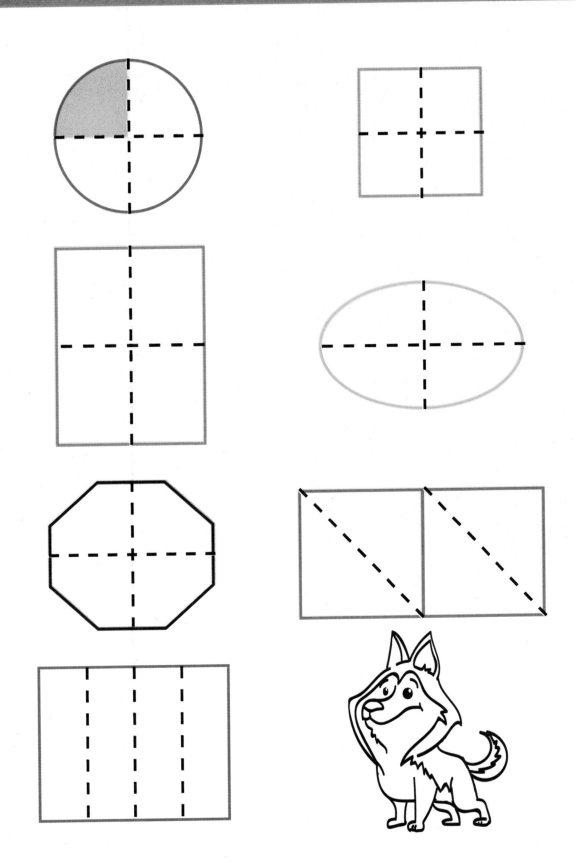

Colour $\frac{1}{2}$ of each of the shapes below. The first one is done for you.

Learning Goal: Recognize fractions shand be able to create them using shapes.

76

Colour $\frac{1}{2}$ of each set of objects below. The first one is done for you.

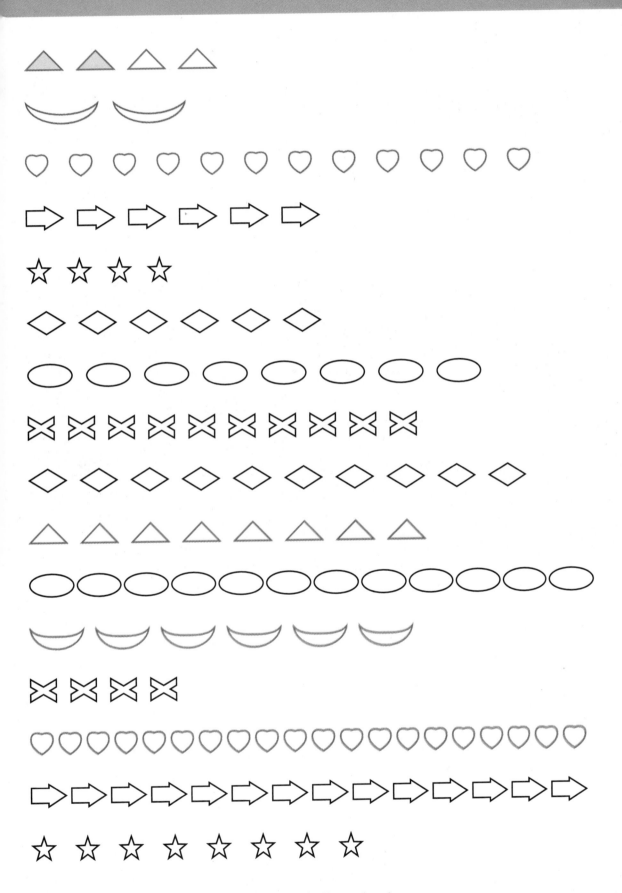

Learning Goal: Recognize fractions and be able to create them using shapes.

77

Colour the shapes and groups below so they match the fractions. The first one is done for you.

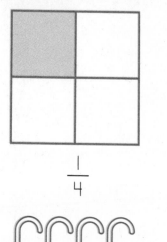

$\dfrac{1}{4}$

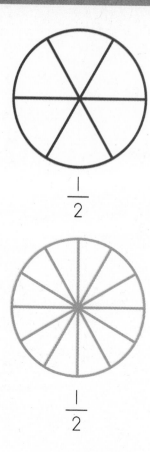

$\dfrac{1}{2}$

$\dfrac{1}{2}$

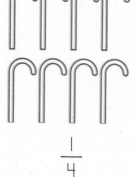

$\dfrac{1}{4}$

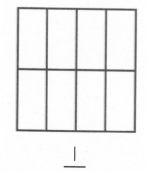

$\dfrac{1}{2}$

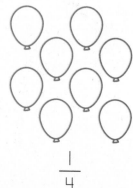

$\dfrac{1}{2}$

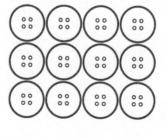

$\dfrac{1}{4}$

$\dfrac{1}{4}$

$\dfrac{1}{4}$

$\dfrac{1}{2}$

$\dfrac{1}{4}$

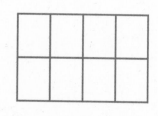

$\dfrac{1}{4}$

Learning Goal: Recognize fractions and be able to create them using shapes.

Colour the shapes and groups below so they match the fractions.

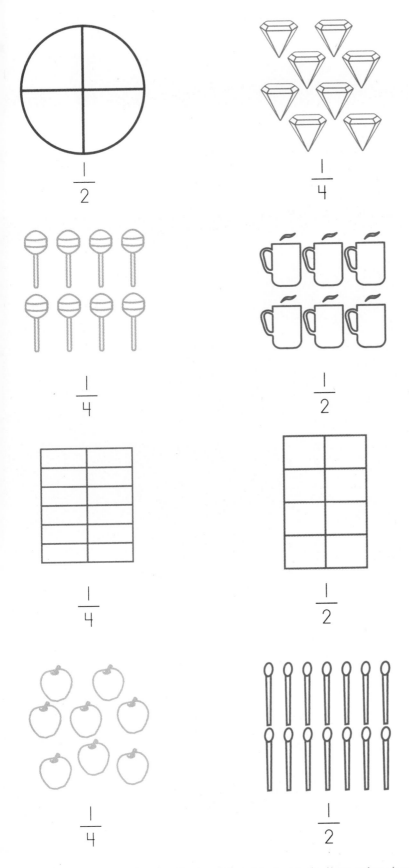

$\frac{1}{2}$

$\frac{1}{4}$

$\frac{1}{4}$

$\frac{1}{4}$

$\frac{1}{2}$

$\frac{1}{4}$

$\frac{1}{4}$

$\frac{1}{2}$

$\frac{1}{2}$

$\frac{1}{4}$

$\frac{1}{2}$

$\frac{1}{4}$

Learning Goal: Recognize fractions and be able to create them using shapes.

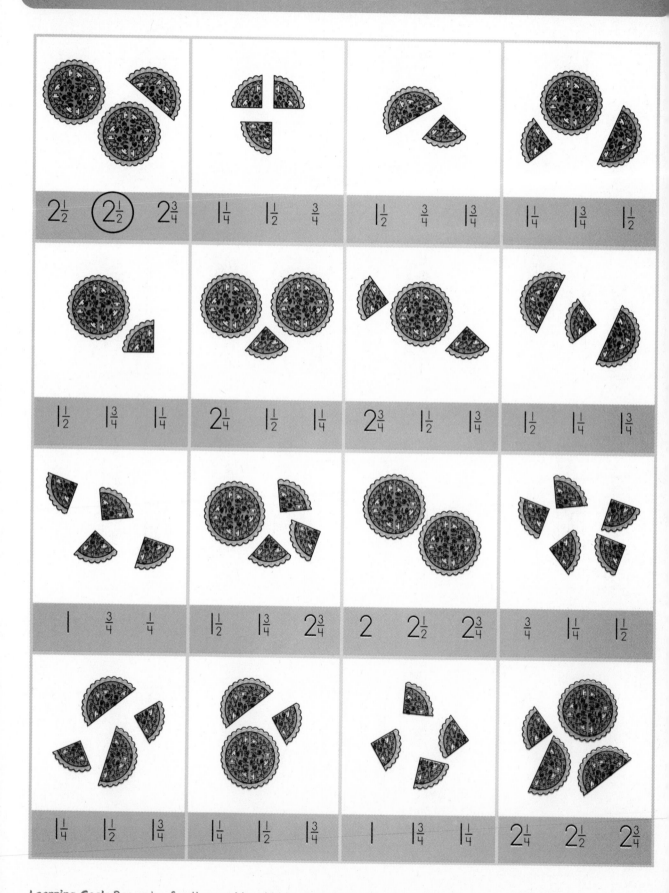

Row 1:
$2\frac{1}{2}$ ⊘$2\frac{1}{2}$ $2\frac{3}{4}$ | $1\frac{1}{4}$ $1\frac{1}{2}$ $\frac{3}{4}$ | $1\frac{1}{2}$ $\frac{3}{4}$ $1\frac{3}{4}$ | $1\frac{1}{4}$ $1\frac{3}{4}$ $1\frac{1}{2}$

Row 2:
$1\frac{1}{2}$ $1\frac{3}{4}$ $1\frac{1}{4}$ | $2\frac{1}{4}$ $1\frac{1}{2}$ $1\frac{1}{4}$ | $2\frac{3}{4}$ $1\frac{1}{2}$ $1\frac{3}{4}$ | $1\frac{1}{2}$ $1\frac{1}{4}$ $1\frac{3}{4}$

Row 3:
1 $\frac{3}{4}$ $\frac{1}{4}$ | $1\frac{1}{2}$ $1\frac{3}{4}$ $2\frac{3}{4}$ | 2 $2\frac{1}{2}$ $2\frac{3}{4}$ | $\frac{3}{4}$ $1\frac{1}{4}$ $1\frac{1}{2}$

Row 4:
$1\frac{1}{4}$ $1\frac{1}{2}$ $1\frac{3}{4}$ | $1\frac{1}{4}$ $1\frac{1}{2}$ $1\frac{3}{4}$ | 1 $\frac{3}{4}$ $1\frac{1}{4}$ | $2\frac{1}{4}$ $2\frac{1}{2}$ $2\frac{3}{4}$

Learning Goal: Recognize fractions and be able to correctly match shapes to corresponding fractions.

80

Look at the pizzas below and circle the correct fraction. The first one is done for you.

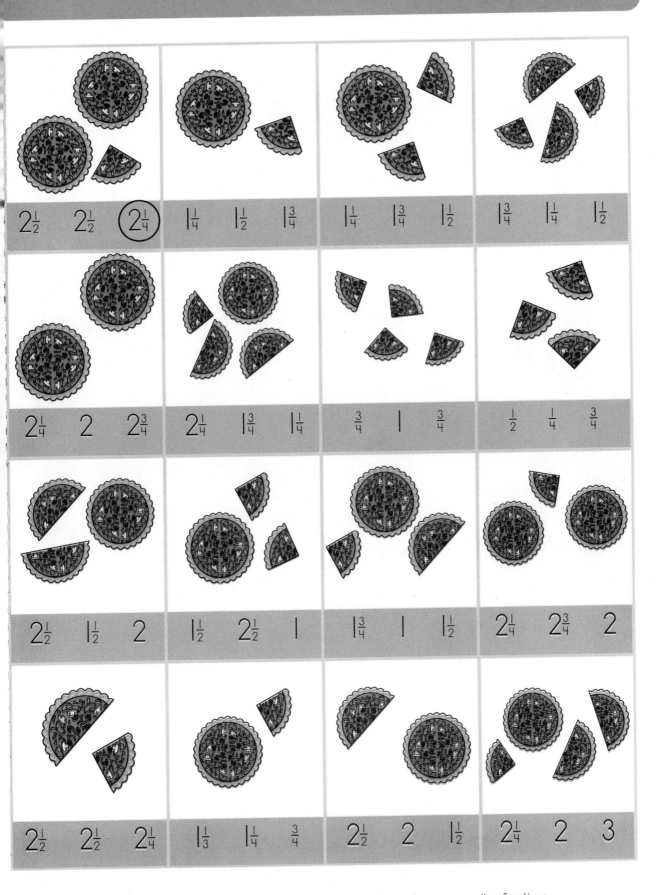

| $2\frac{1}{2}$ | $2\frac{1}{2}$ | ⊛$2\frac{1}{4}$⊛ | $1\frac{1}{4}$ | $1\frac{1}{2}$ | $1\frac{3}{4}$ | $1\frac{1}{4}$ | $1\frac{3}{4}$ | $1\frac{1}{2}$ | $1\frac{3}{4}$ | $1\frac{1}{4}$ | $1\frac{1}{2}$ |

| $2\frac{1}{4}$ | 2 | $2\frac{3}{4}$ | $2\frac{1}{4}$ | $1\frac{3}{4}$ | $1\frac{1}{4}$ | $\frac{3}{4}$ | 1 | $\frac{3}{4}$ | $\frac{1}{2}$ | $\frac{1}{4}$ | $\frac{3}{4}$ |

| $2\frac{1}{2}$ | $1\frac{1}{2}$ | 2 | $1\frac{1}{2}$ | $2\frac{1}{2}$ | 1 | $1\frac{3}{4}$ | 1 | $1\frac{1}{2}$ | $2\frac{1}{4}$ | $2\frac{3}{4}$ | 2 |

| $2\frac{1}{2}$ | $2\frac{1}{2}$ | $2\frac{1}{4}$ | $1\frac{1}{3}$ | $1\frac{1}{4}$ | $\frac{3}{4}$ | $2\frac{1}{2}$ | 2 | $1\frac{1}{2}$ | $2\frac{1}{4}$ | 2 | 3 |

Learning Goal: Recognize fractions and be able to correctly match shapes to corresponding fractions.

Solve the fraction addition problems below by writing the number of coloured parts on the lines below each shape. The first one is done for you.

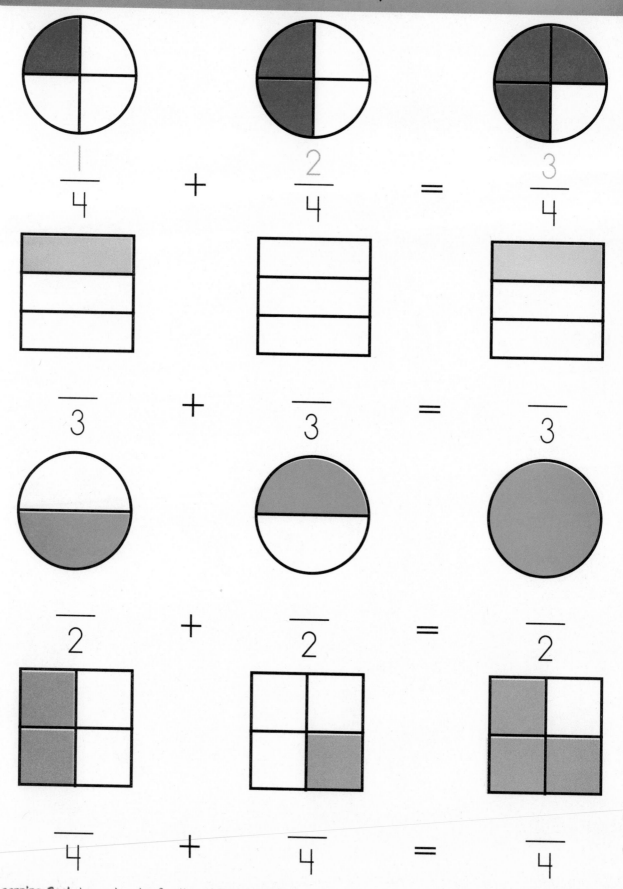

$$\frac{1}{4} \quad + \quad \frac{2}{4} \quad = \quad \frac{3}{4}$$

$$\frac{}{3} \quad + \quad \frac{}{3} \quad = \quad \frac{}{3}$$

$$\frac{}{2} \quad + \quad \frac{}{2} \quad = \quad \frac{}{2}$$

$$\frac{}{4} \quad + \quad \frac{}{4} \quad = \quad \frac{}{4}$$

Learning Goal: Learn to solve fraction addition problems.

Solve the fraction subtraction problems below by writing the number of coloured parts on the lines below each shape. The first one is done for you.

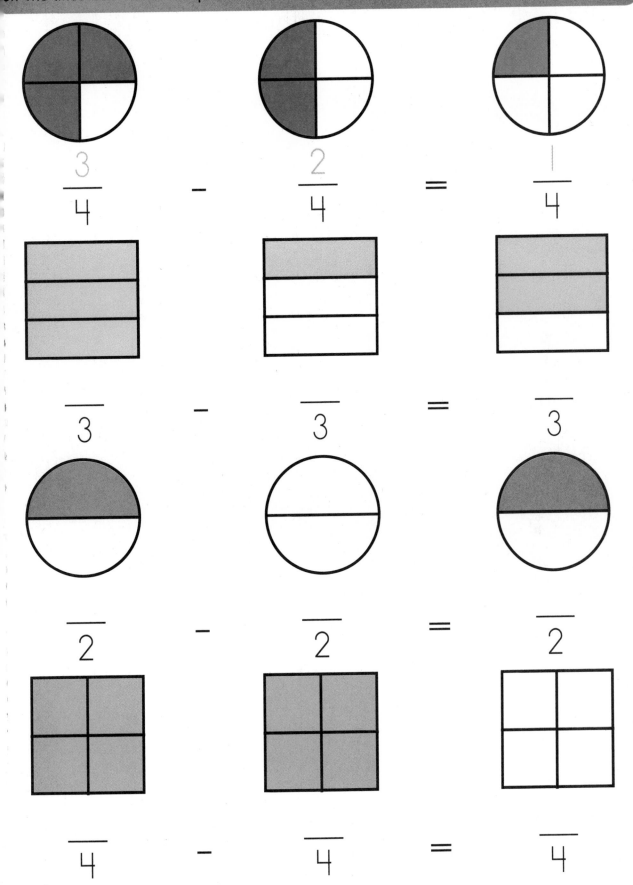

$$\frac{3}{4} \quad - \quad \frac{2}{4} \quad = \quad \frac{1}{4}$$

$$\frac{}{3} \quad - \quad \frac{}{3} \quad = \quad \frac{}{3}$$

$$\frac{}{2} \quad - \quad \frac{}{2} \quad = \quad \frac{}{2}$$

$$\frac{}{4} \quad - \quad \frac{}{4} \quad = \quad \frac{}{4}$$

Learning Goal: Learn to solve fraction subtraction problems.

Learn the names of 3-D shapes by tracing the word and then writing it on your own.

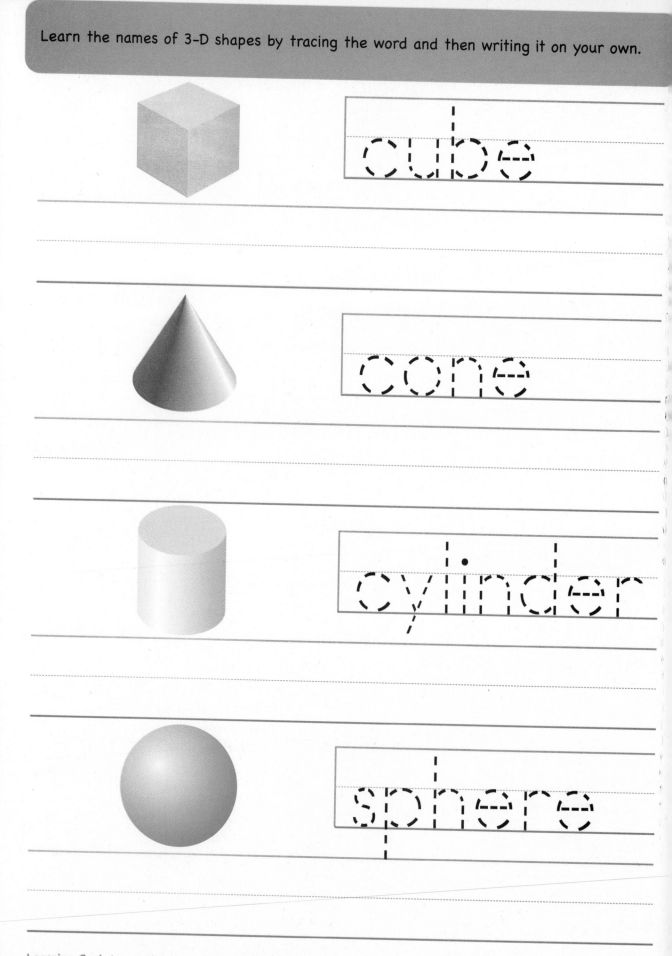

Learning Goal: Learn about common 3-D shapes.

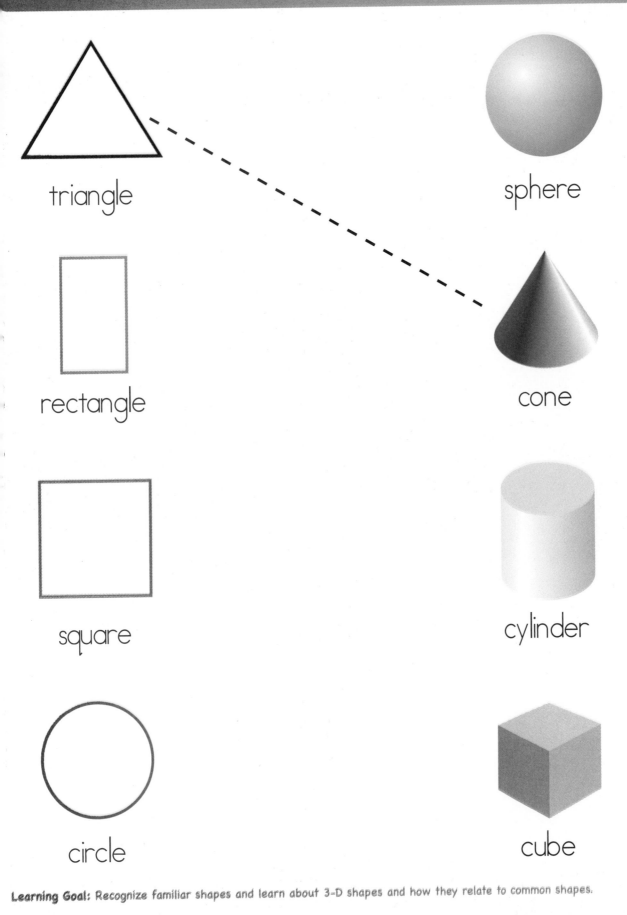

triangle

sphere

rectangle

cone

square

cylinder

circle

cube

Learning Goal: Recognize familiar shapes and learn about 3-D shapes and how they relate to common shapes.

Cubes have six sides. Circle the number 6 in the cube.

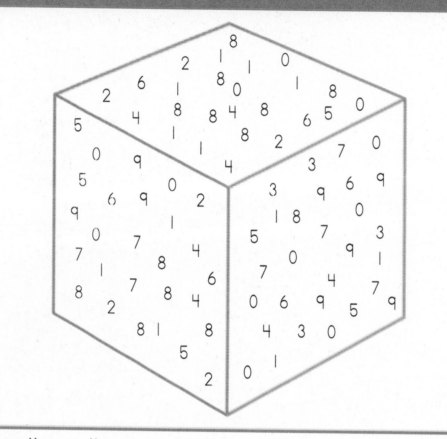

Solve the equations on the cone and add the total number of scoops. The first one is done for you.

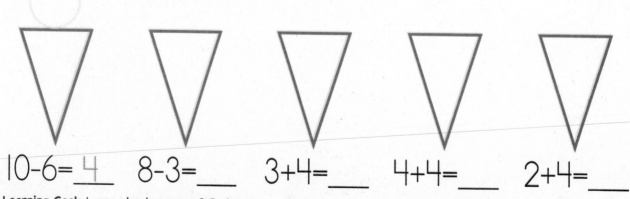

$10-6=\underline{4}$ $8-3=\underline{}$ $3+4=\underline{}$ $4+4=\underline{}$ $2+4=\underline{}$

Learning Goal: Learn about common 3-D shapes.

Draw 4 more cylinders to place logs under the fire.

Colour each sphere to make it look like a planet.

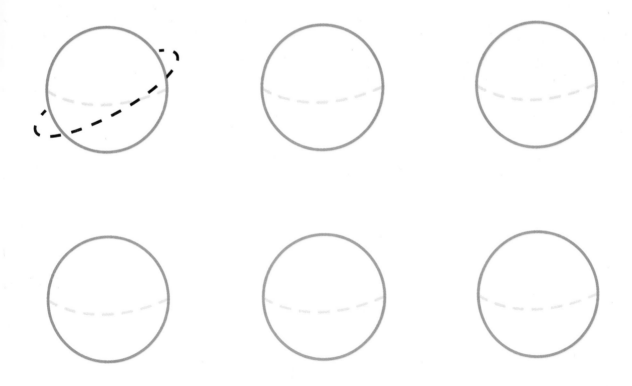

Follow the directions below to help the goalie find the puck.

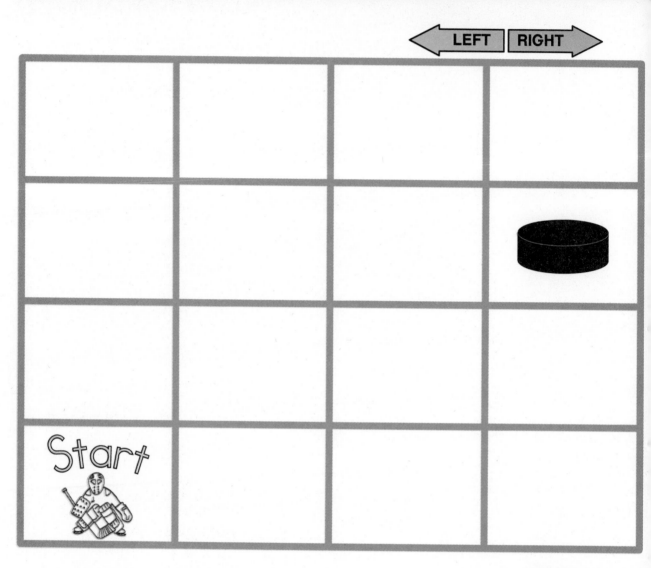

LEFT | RIGHT

Start

1. Move two boxes to the right.

2. Go up one box.

3. Move one box to the left.

4. Go up one box.

5. Move two boxes to the right.

Follow the directions below to help the bunny find a carrot.

North

West

East

START

South

1. Move two blocks to the east.
2. Move three blocks to the north.
3. Move one block to the west.
4. Move two blocks to the south.
5. Move three blocks to the east.
6. Move two blocks to the north to find a carrot.

Use the grid to fill in the blanks with north, south, east, or west.

1. The bee is to the _____ of the flower.

2. The grass is to the _____ of the bee.

3. The butterfly is to the _____ of the grass.

4. The bee is to the _____ of the grass.

Use the grid to answer the questions. Write your answers on the lines below.

1. What is east of the butterfly? _____

2. What is south of the flower? _____

3. What is west of the flower? _____

Learning Goal: Read and use positional vocabulary relevantly.

Use the grid to answer the questions below.

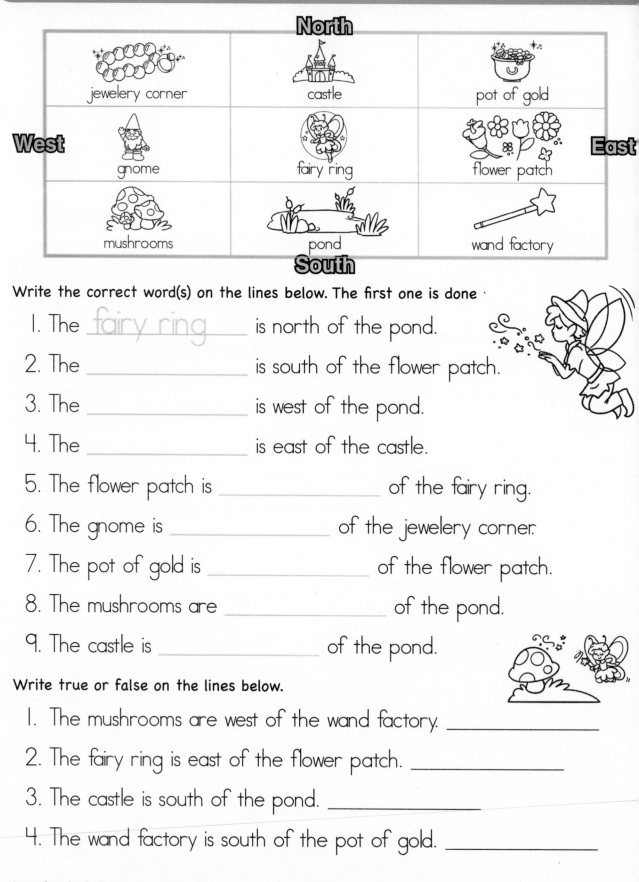

Write the correct word(s) on the lines below. The first one is done

1. The _fairy ring_ is north of the pond.

2. The _____ is south of the flower patch.

3. The _____ is west of the pond.

4. The _____ is east of the castle.

5. The flower patch is _____ of the fairy ring.

6. The gnome is _____ of the jewelery corner.

7. The pot of gold is _____ of the flower patch.

8. The mushrooms are _____ of the pond.

9. The castle is _____ of the pond.

Write true or false on the lines below.

1. The mushrooms are west of the wand factory. _____

2. The fairy ring is east of the flower patch. _____

3. The castle is south of the pond. _____

4. The wand factory is south of the pot of gold. _____

Learning Goal: Read and write positional vocabulary accurately.

4 kangaroos	3 dogs	2 zebras	2 pigs	2 tigers

1. How many animals do you count?

Kangaroos	4
Dogs	
Zebras	
Pigs	
Tigers	
Total	

2. Which animals have stripes? _____ and _____

3. How many legs

   (a) does one pig have?   _____

   (b) do all the pigs have?   _____

4. How many legs

   (a) does one dog have?   _____

   (b) do all the dogs have?   _____

5. How many ears

   (a) does one zebra have?   _____

   (b) do all the zebras have?   _____

Learning Goal: Read and select the correct option.

Colour the picture. Then find and circle the following objects: 8 starfish, 9 lobsters, 16 seashells, 4 crabs, 21 bubbles, 13 fish, and 2 boats.

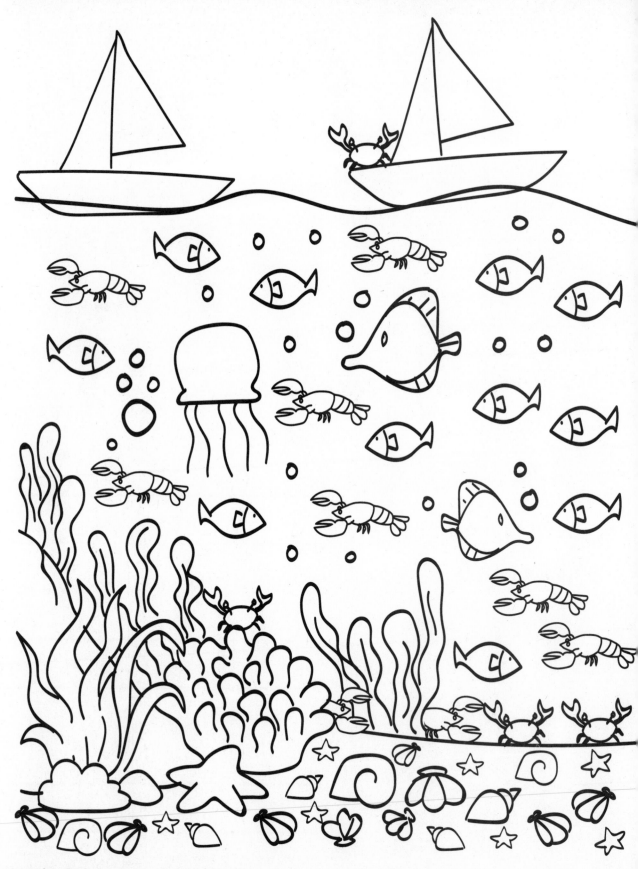

Learning Goal: Read and respond to directions.

Spot the differences in the pictures. Circle each one.

Learning Goal: Read and respond to directions.

Solve the problems below. Then match the letters to the numbers on the bottom of the page to reveal a secret message.

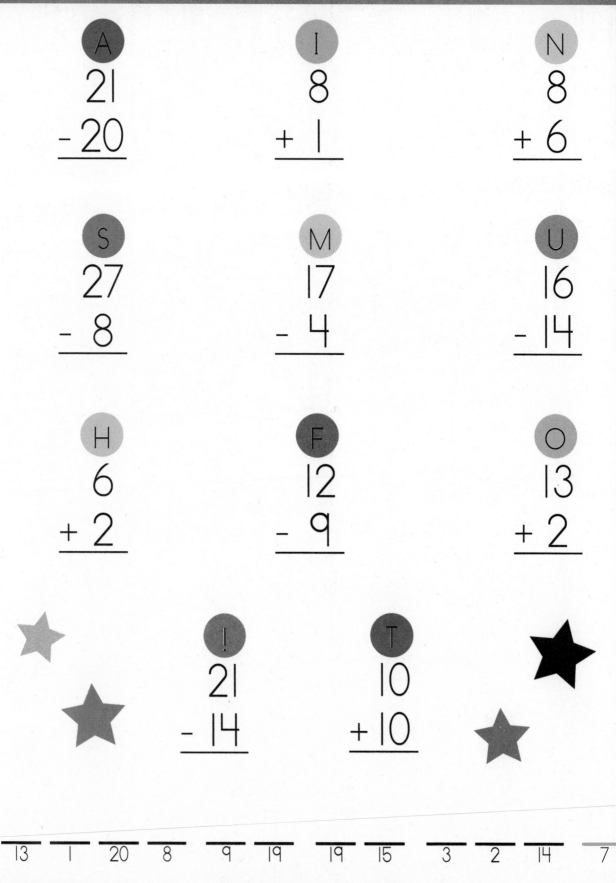

A
21
- 20

I
8
+ 1

N
8
+ 6

S
27
- 8

M
17
- 4

U
16
- 14

H
6
+ 2

F
12
- 9

O
13
+ 2

!
21
- 14

T
10
+ 10

___ ___ ___ ___   ___ ___   ___ ___   ___ ___ ___ ___   ___
13   1   20   8   9   19   19   15   3   2   14   7

Solve the problems below. Then match the letters to the numbers on the bottom of the page to reveal a secret message.

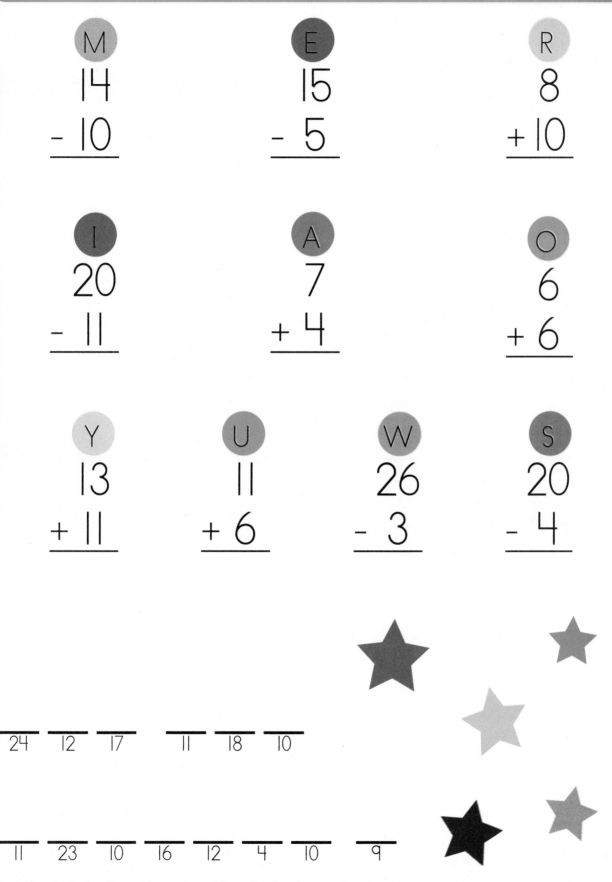

M
14
- 10

E
15
- 5

R
8
+ 10

I
20
- 11

A
7
+ 4

O
6
+ 6

Y
13
+ 11

U
11
+ 6

W
26
- 3

S
20
- 4

___ ___ ___   ___ ___ ___
24   12   17   11   18   10

___ ___ ___ ___ ___ ___ ___   ___
11   23   10   16   12   4   10   9

Learning Goal: Practice solving math problems. Read and respond to directions.

A GREAT CANADIAN WORKBOOK

CONGRATULATIONS!

This is to certify that

_____
Name

has completed Grade One Math!

Date: _____

1 2 3 4 5 6 7 8 9 10